May this book bless you Alway.

Ruth D. [signature]

One Night

One Night

Keith D. Jenkins

Library of Congress Control Number: 2017912258
ISBN: Hardcover   978-1-5434-4266-3
                   Softcover   978-1-5434-4267-0
                   eBook   978-1-5434-4268-7

Print information available on the last page.

Rev. date: 10/13/2017

To order additional copies of this book, contact:
Xlibris
1-888-795-4274
www.Xlibris.com
Orders@Xlibris.com
759645

Table of Contents

PART I
GENESIS

PART II
GROWING UP

PART III
MY GIFT

PART IV
REHABILITATION

PART V
RECOVERY

WORDS FROM THE AUTHOR

THE PURPOSE AND intent of this book isn't to expose my business but to share my story of how love rehabilitated me. Love inspired me; it encouraged me to overcome my addiction to alcohol and became my biggest motivator. Love became my focus; I went from being an alcoholic and a deadbeat dad, to a father, husband, and an ordained minister all through the blessing of love. Please take this journey with me through my story.

-Keith D. Jenkins

FOREWORD

WHEN YOU TOLD me five years ago you wanted to write your story, my reply was, "Keith, I'm not going to write it for you". And that was the end of the conversation. I knew had I said "Let me help you", then they would have been my words and not yours. I wanted to make sure it was your voice that was being heard and your story that was being told. Over the next five years, I saw your struggles as they all played out. You wrote, you wrestled with thoughts, you cried, you got depressed. I saw all of the emotions that this book brought out of you. I know it was difficult for you because it took you to some places that you wanted to leave buried. But you knew God wanted this story to be told. At times it took you away from spending time with me and the boys, but you were lost in your thoughts and committed to getting this work completed. There is a message here for someone that needs deliverance in this area. So thank you for your obedience, diligence, and commitment to his charge. I'm very proud of you and what you have accomplished.

Your loving wife,
Tina

PROLOGUE

A S WE DROVE along, we were talking and laughing and overall just enjoying the day. I was behind the wheel, going at a normal pace, not speeding at all. Typically when I drove I had a beer in my lap, and this day was no different. As we were driving along, out of nowhere, a sudden gust of wind airlifted the car. It went flying nose-first, then flipped backwards, and finally landed on its hood, crushing all of us. We were killed upon impact.

PART I

GENESIS

It's at the start of your life where you're most impressionable. The things that transpire set the foundation that shapes and develops you into the person you're going to be. It doesn't mean that if your foundation isn't strong, you won't survive adversity, it just means that if you find cracks and they aren't addressed quickly, they may cause long-term damage.

-Keith D. Jenkins

DREAMS

J UST LIKE ANY other child, I had bad dreams. They made it difficult for me to sleep. The dreams were not your ordinary Boogieman or Freddie Krueger type of dreams. I was not having them because I had just watched something scary on TV. Oftentimes, the dreams would have me afraid to sleep which led to many sleepless nights. During the day I was be restless because I had nothing but thoughts from the dreams. The best way I can explain my dreams is that they took my mind to very dark places.

As the dreams began, I saw images of people that were pitch black. They were blacker than any shade of black I had ever seen before. Their scariest feature were their eyes. They had reddish pink shifty eyes with irises that never stopped moving. These images haunted my dreams and I felt as if they were always following me around. The dreams took place in really dark places. The scariest dreams were so dark it felt like I was in hell. In these places I would hear these images crying out nonstop. The sounds were quite disturbing. This was very scary and unnerving to an eight year old which was about the age I was when I started having the dreams. In my dreams the images could talk but they had no mouth. I would hear them speak when I made eye contact with them which I tried to avoid because I was terrified of them. As a small child I would always dream of them. Every night as I closed my eyes, I was afraid to fall asleep waiting on the images to visit me in my dreams. At some point, my dreams became a reality and I found myself constantly surrounded by the images and the cries. They were loud and unpredictable and would appear out of nowhere.

School was a place where I needed peace and quiet so that I could I focus on my studies, but I would hear the voices there as well. These voices had no boundaries and often I would hear them more than I heard the teachers. At times the voices would say negative things directly to me, other times it was just background noise that sounded like a lot of conversations going on all at once. With all the noise going on in my head and the lack of sleep at night, I was a very angry and scared child. I couldn't go to my parents with this because no one would believe me. I had no outlet, so I chose to act out. This was the only way I felt I could deal with this problem. Acting out only led to negative feedback from my teachers and so called friends. They would talk about me and say things like "You dumb as hell" or "You can't do what other kids do". These comments were hurtful and made me feel sad, as if I wasn't normal and as if I didn't fit in with the other kids. Because I had to deal with the images and the voices in my dreams that were now stalking me in my daily life, I didn't feel normal. I had other challenges as well. I wanted to run and play with others, but my weight was a problem too. Kids were cruel so my early childhood struggles with obesity definitely didn't help in my fight to fit in and feel normal. The voices would taunt me and remind me of my past attempts to fit in and my failures. "You're just like us–A failure" was what I would often hear. But the images and the voices would never explain why they were haunting me or why I continued to see them in my dreams.

I remember one dream quite vividly. It started with me waking up in an operating room. There was a doctor and the scary black images present. The doctor had just performed surgery. The peculiar thing about the doctor was that he was much larger than the other images, and he had his back to me as if he didn't want to be seen. He said, "With your new heart and mind, I can control you from here". What appeared to be a heart and a brain lying next to me looked like a surgery gone wrong. According to the scary dark image that spoke to me, it was a successful procedure. The thing that I remembered most about this dream was that after the removal of my heart and brain there was applause, in fact, the loudest I had ever heard from the other scary figures in the room.

I was unsure why I was having the dreams but I didn't tell anyone about them because I knew no one would believe me. How do you sit down with your parents at the age of eight and have this conversation? Who would believe you? Even if they did what would happen? A trip to the psychiatrist and medicated for the rest of my life. I can't really say I had thought through all of these as solutions to this problem at that age, but I didn't think I could tell my parents or anyone for that matter. I didn't want anyone to think I was crazy because I knew I wasn't. I wasn't sure what was going on with me or why I was having the dreams or why I was hearing and seeing these images.

The dreams impaired me in so many ways, but school was where I experienced my most difficult struggles. I found myself sleeping a lot in class. I would sit in the back with my head on my desk. My teachers encouraged me to try to rest at night because school was not the place to sleep. I guess I rested well in class because school was noisy; the noise helped drown out the voices. Unlike school, the house was too quiet at night so I couldn't sleep because all I would hear were the voices.

As a result of sleeping during class, I was failing academically. I was struggling with basic reading, writing, and math skills, but was keeping it hidden from my parents for as long as I could. One day a teacher asked me to read aloud to the class, frustrated because I was always sleeping in her class; she wanted to see if I was paying attention. Everybody started to laugh and I felt embarrassed; I got extremely angry and lashed out and said, "B****h I can't read this s**t. You read it!"

She was very surprised at my language as well as disappointed in my behavior. She said, "Go to the principal's office!"

Again, I lashed out, "I ain't going no damn where!"

The reaction from the class was met with applause much like what I had experienced in my earlier dream. She on the other hand was noticeably upset and almost in tears. I knew she was disappointed at what I had said, and I knew what I had said was wrong, but for some reason, I didn't care. I was angry and my outburst allowed me to release that anger. Unfortunately my little stunt got me fast tracked straight to the principal's office. This would be one of many trips to the office for disruptive behavior. "Keith, I'm disappointed in you because I know this is not you" was what the principal said to me which made me want to cry. I felt like he knew I wasn't acting like myself. God knows I wanted to tell him what I was dealing with in my dreams but I didn't, because I honestly felt like no one would believe me.

The older I got the more traumatic the dreams became. At this point, sleep was unattainable and my behavior had spiraled out of control. I felt like I didn't have the ability to learn and quite frankly no one wanted to deal with me anyway. My behavior was the real issue but it was a distraction in a futile attempt to the cover up the fact that I couldn't read or write. There were multiple attempts to try to get me back on track, but the final recommendation was to place me in Special Education. My parents did not want me there, and I certainly did not want to go, but I left them no choice.

Going into the fifth grade, I was disappointed because for the first time in our lives my twin brother and I were going to different schools. I was devastated. Change can be scary and not having Kenneth, who we call Kenny, at the same school was hard for me. The school that I was attending had a Special Education program set up for kids with behavioral problems that placed an emphasis on behavior. This school was not good for me. Their focus was on behavior and not learning disabilities which was what I needed. Everyone expected the move to set me on the right track, but instead of getting better, I got worse. I spent a lot of time in and out of the principal's office and one teacher went so far as to say I was a "problem child". About mid-year I was moved to yet another school that focused even more on behavior issues. By the time it was time to enroll in middle school, I had gone to four different elementary schools.

FAMILY

I DIDN'T GROW up in a classic American family with a mother, father, two kids and a dog. There were six of us and we had a strong family bond. But because there were a lot of mouths to feed, my parents worked a lot. My mom worked to support us, at times maintaining up to four jobs at once. She taught us the value of hard work. It was important to her that we had what we needed so even if it took four jobs to have it, that's what she did. My mom was the bright spot in our home, always maintaining a smile. I know she had a lot she dealt with but she internalized most things. I really wanted to confide in her to tell her what I was dealing with because she was my biggest supporter, but she had enough on her plate. I didn't want to burden her with my issues with the dreams. That would require even more out of her when she was already stretched so thin just trying to keep our household together. We weren't the perfect family, but she did what she could to make our home as perfect as it could be. I appreciated her for that. It was a struggle because of my dad and his habit. My dad was a good father but he had an addiction that took him away from his responsibilities. He did what he could to help but the bulk of his money went to his habit. Despite that, he taught us morals and values and didn't stand for any disrespect. Because we had two working parents, they were away from the house a lot. When we were not in school we were left to see about ourselves which meant me and my brothers spent a lot of time together.

There were four of us, Charles and Bobby were the two oldest. They were about ten years older than Kenny and I. They were practically twins, only about eleven months apart. The thing I loved most about my older brothers was that they were close. Our parents instilled that in us. We had to look out for each other. Charles and Bobby made sure no one messed with Kenny and I and taught us how to defend ourselves. We were our brother's keepers. Because Charles and Bobby were so much older than us and had moved out the house, it was just Kenny and I during most of our adolescent years. We were fraternal twins and there was a special bond between us. Kenny was always a little sickly suffering from really bad asthma as a child. I was the oldest twin so I felt like I was his protector. It was my responsibility to watch over him as much as possible. No one said I had to take on this role, and Kenny never knew I thought of myself in this light.

I remember on one occasion I was in afterschool detention and Kenny was outside waiting on me to be released so that we could walk home together. I had a few more minutes left in class when I heard someone say "Ain't that Kenny coming, get him!" Immediately my ears shot out and I was on my feet running. The next thing I knew I was down the hall toward the exit. As I exited the building, I saw Kenny fighting so I joined in to help. That's how close we were. If you messed with one, you messed with both of us. There was no such thing as his fight and my fight. There was no way I was going to sit around and spectate. After our win, we walked home celebrating. We made no mention of this event to our parents so I'm not even sure that they ever knew this happened.

Kenny and I were as close as any two brothers could be. I just had this secret between us that I hated. I loved my brother as well as the rest of my family. I really felt like the outcast though because I was different. They didn't treat me differently because no one really knew my struggles, but I knew. How could I tell them? They were all dealing with their own struggles. I didn't need to weigh them down with my issues as well.

EATING DISORDER

ENTERING MIDDLE SCHOOL, eating became another issue. The more I ate, the better I felt. The better I felt, the larger I got. I found comfort in food resulting in a different problem. I found myself overeating at both school and at home. I would eat all the food the other kids at school didn't want and at home I overate because my parents were always working and not there to oversee our dinners. No one was there to tell me not to go for the second and third serving that I didn't need. Although I found some satisfaction in my gluttonous ways, the overeating didn't change or stop the dreams. By now, I was beginning to learn to live with them and the voices.

My weight had spiraled out of control by the time my parents noticed and decided to do something about it. This is when they took me to the doctor to get a medical diagnosis. The doctor explained my condition as emotional eating. He said that a lot of kids ate emotionally which is why I gained weight so quickly, topping out at about two hundred fifteen pounds in middle school. My dad, being the cut and dry kind of person that he was, said the problem was, "I ate too damn much." While the doctor didn't disagree, he still insisted it was triggered by my emotions and recommended admitting me into the hospital. He felt that it was more than just eating. He was right, but there was no way I could tell them what was truly causing me to overeat. He knew something was triggering the eating disorder and hopefully a stay in the hospital would reveal what the cause was. I stayed a week only to find out the weight gain did in fact come from emotional eating. The doctor put me on a thousand-calorie a day diet; it helped with my weight but did nothing for the problem. I was told to play more and make healthier food choices. None of the advice that the doctor gave me helped me mentally; it only explained why I was fat.

Being a fat kid wasn't easy. What made it more difficult were the physical differences between me and my twin. It was really tough growing up and hearing people say, I was "eating up all the food from my twin." Some people did not believe we were twins because Kenny was tall and skinny and I was short and fat. They nicknamed us "Skinny Kenny and Fat Keith". This would make me really angry. I remember always running to tell my older brothers when someone would say something bad about me. My brothers said I needed to toughen up and told me that if I told them about somebody picking on me one more time, they would whip me. You definitely had to have thick skin growing up in our house. No one was going to pacify you because no one had time for that. I had to learn this lesson very early in life. Eventually I got fed up with being picked on and learned to defend myself. Instead of getting whipped, I learned to start fighting back verbally.

I was always getting into some type of trouble and the summer of my eighth grade year was no different. It was the summer that I ran away from home. My parents suspected me of smoking cigarettes because I would smell like cigarette smoke, but they didn't have any proof. They would ask, "Why do you smell like smoke?" or "Have you been smoking?" My answer would always be, "I don't know," or "No." On this particular day, I was in the back bedroom standing at the window smoking; my parents were not home. Anytime I was smoking in the house, I would always blow the smoke out the window to keep down the smell. I had to listen closely for my parents or older brothers in case they walked in. For one reason or another, on this particular day, I didn't hear my dad come home. He walked right in and caught me!

There was nothing I could say. To say he was pissed off would be putting it mildly. He was outraged. But as I stood there holding the cigarette, he calmly stated, "You do smoke huh? Go ahead and finish and when you're done, I'mma deal with you."

I always thought my dad was funny, but clearly I was not going to experience any ha-ha, laugh it up moments with my dad right now. Now was not the time he was going to be funny! I knew I was not getting out of this one; there was a punishment I would have to face. I had a beatdown coming. Now they knew I had lied, and that was not going to help my case either. After weighing all my options, there was only one thing I could do. When my dad turned and walked towards his bedroom, I ran. He yelled, "Keith, come here, boy! Don't you run from me!"

I probably wouldn't have run had he just whipped me immediately after he caught me. He wanted to spark fear in me, which he did. That's what parents do when they make you think about your whipping before they actually give it to you. I don't think he thought I would flee though. After he told me to finish my cigarette then he would handle me stressed me out. All I could think about was the beating that was coming, so I ran. I don't know why I ran, but I did. My dad tried to catch me but couldn't. I knew once he caught me it was going to be bad, so I stayed away for several hours. Kenny and a neighborhood friend were worried and came looking for me. Because they were a lot smaller than me and physically in better shape, they were able to catchup with me and bring me home; to the punishment that awaited me.

By the time we made it home, my mom was there as well. I thought I was going to be okay because my mom was home. She would save me. She would protect me from my father's wrath. My dad was noticeably upset, cursing, and explaining to my mom what happened. He let my mom know the reason I was getting the whipping. It was because I lied! I don't know if my dad had a change of heart, but he didn't whip me and that was surprising. Whew, I thought I was in the clear. Unfortunately, my mom was not in the same forgiving spirit this evening. She made it very clear, "You're getting this because you got caught smoking and lied to me and your father." I think deep down my parents felt something else was causing all the issues but didn't know what needed to be addressed. They knew that there was something causing me to act out. They told me that if I didn't straighten myself out, they would look into putting me in a reform school, which was a school for wayward kids. *God, not another school and another change.* This was definitely not what I wanted.

HIGH SCHOOL

A LTHOUGH I MOVED from junior high to high school, I didn't feel like I had accomplished anything. I guess because I was still in Special Ed. I honestly felt like Special Education was a babysitter. There was no work to actually push me, and there was nothing to challenge me. The reality was I didn't need to be there. Being in those type of classes left me no choice but to act out. I wanted to learn, and in fact, I knew I could. Basic concepts just took me longer to get than others. This didn't mean I didn't have the ability to learn. I just had to put in more work. Because everyone was so focused on my behavior issues, they overshadowed my ability or lack thereof to learn.

High school brought on new challenges, new beginnings, and for most students, it was exciting times. Most kids enjoyed their high school days. For me it was humiliating. I was embarrassed to be in Special Ed. It brought with it the stigma of being a dummy but also it separated Kenny and I from being in classes together. High school left me feeling empty and wanting. Other students had goals and plans for the future; they had a purpose and a reason for being in school. With me, I just felt like I was going through the motions. For a long time I would ask myself, "Why me? Why was I the dumb one? Why couldn't I learn and behave like other students?"

Even in high school I was still bothered by the dreams and by this time I had experienced some thoughts of suicide. I felt it was a way to end this hurt and loneliness they were causing. The dreams were silently destroying and slowly killing me. I was an angry child because I couldn't express myself and talk about my problems. The only thing I knew how to do was misbehave. My new title with the administrative staff was now "problem child", a label that I was familiar with. This was just my cover-up because I was dealing with a lot of stuff at this stage in my life; the dreams, Special Ed, and my weight which was now up to two hundred and fifty pounds. I'm sure all of the people who were judging me would have changed their opinions of me had they known what I was dealing with.

I will say High School wasn't all that bad. There was one activity in school that helped me feel normal. If it wasn't for my love of music and being a member of the marching band, I'm not sure how I would have made it. Band was the one thing that helped me feel like I belonged to something. It was meaningful and allowed me to fit in. It also provided some light at the end of a very dark tunnel.

Outside of participating in the band, there was nothing to motivate me to get up and go to school on a daily basis. I knew I had to, but I had nothing to look forward to in Special Education. I wasn't being taught anything to prepare me for a future after high school. My future after Special Ed was going to be survival. There was no way I would excel with the tools I was getting. What I observed at school was, some teachers taught to prepare you for the next academic level, while others taught you based on the level you were on. Some accepted where you were and would allow you to do just enough to get by but others pushed you to the next level. I wanted more; I just didn't know how to go about getting it. Because of where I was at this stage in my high school career, I didn't think I was entitled to an education, not the same education I saw others students getting so I made a decision. In my eleventh grade year I talked to my parents about dropping out of school. I felt it wasn't in my best interest to continue. There was no future on this road I was traveling on as far as education was concerned. I wasn't going to college because Special Ed kids didn't go to college. This was a waste of my time. Of course my parents adamantly disagreed with me and still continued to encourage me to work harder. For them, *quitting was not an option.*

In high school, I noticed was there were many students dealing with a number of issues. Everyone had a coping mechanism for dealing with their problems as well as perspective on how you might want to handle yours. Of course it was up to the individual to figure out their own issues, but nevertheless, everyone found a way to deal with them. Some students used sports or other activities to help keep them busy. As for me, the band became my outlet to keep my mind occupied. These were ways most students worked through their problems. Unfortunately for others, coping came through the use of drugs and alcohol.

One of the things I find interesting about kids is that generally speaking they will share their problems with other kids, probably before they would choose to confide in an adult. It was not uncommon for students to talk to each other. While I found it difficult to open up to my parents and even my siblings about my dreams, I found it easy on one particular day to share with a kid I was in the band with. I remember talking to him about how I had been having bad dreams since I was a little kid and how it made it hard to sleep. I told him that some of the dreams I had couldn't be explained and they didn't make sense. We talked about in one dream where I shook hands with the devil and in another where I had done something terrible and didn't ask for forgiveness. I was never myself in my dreams. I was doing things I know I would not do. So, I asked him "How do you deal with the stuff you have to deal with?" He later explained his situation and how he was coping with it. He said he knew his situation wasn't going to get any better, and how it was never ending. The way he dealt with his situation was–he got drunk every night.

When he explained his situation to me, he made it seem as if the pain caused by his problems didn't bother him when he drank. The sticking point for me was that he wouldn't feel anything which is how he was able to sleep. I asked, "What do your parents have to say and how do you hide it from them?"

He laughed and said, "Dude, they don't notice me. They are the cause of all my pain!" He had this look on his face like he didn't care what his parents thought.

Out of curiosity I asked, "How does drinking help you to sleep?"

He said, "I drink until I fall asleep." I knew I didn't have this option to drink myself to sleep each night. Besides, I was broke, and wouldn't be able to hide the liquor in the house if I could in fact purchase it.

What was interesting about what he told me was that he used alcohol to help him cope with his problem. It hadn't dawned on me that the purpose of drinking was to help cope with a problem. I just assumed when I saw people drinking it was because they actually liked the taste. I had experimented with alcohol before but only to taste but nothing beyond that. But what he said made me curious and I wanted to experiment as well, but I had concerns. What would happen if I tried to fix a problem with something that had the potential to make the problem worse? I knew first hand that the matter could definitely get worse. For a while I went back and forth entertaining the thought and wondering about the "what ifs" of the advice. In the end, the only way to know was that I was going to have to try it.

Purchasing alcohol was about to be a first for me. I had never previously tried to buy it, but I'd seen it done before. From what I knew, the best place to go was the corner store. And, like most neighborhoods, we had one. The folks that worked in the store were well-known by the customers because we saw them frequently. Because we were in and out of the store all the time, the employees knew I was underage. This would generally pose a problem, but fortunately for me, this was not a problem in this store. They would sell to anybody.

I decided to try my luck on a Sunday night. I figured less people would be out. Around eight-thirty I decided to make my move. I was extremely nervous and cautious, but curious at the same time. My mom was getting her uniforms ready for the week; that was her normal routine. She was in the kitchen polishing her shoes for work when I asked, "Mom, can I use the car to go to the store real quick?"

She asked, "At this time of night?" The funny thing is she didn't ask why. She just added, "Hurry up and get back here!"

The drive to the store from our house was about a five-minute drive, but the thoughts going through my mind made it feel longer. I was having thoughts like, *What if someone sees me and tell my parents or what if something bad happens?* While I was worried, none of these thoughts made me not want to go through with it.

There were a few other things that I needed to think through as well. I didn't know what type of beer to buy, which brand, or how much to buy. While I didn't think the fact that I was underage would pose a problem, I didn't want my inexperience in beer buying to bring more attention to me. The reality was I was underage and needed to keep it moving as quickly as I could so that I wouldn't bring attention to myself.

I got to the store and parked so I could do a quick in and out not wanting to be seen. I walked in and spoke to the cashier, looking to see what I could afford.

As if I was a regular, I asked, "What's on sale?"

She said, "The quarts are on sale."

People that I've seen buy quarts don't pick the ones on top; they dig to the bottom of the barrel to get the colder beer. So of course, that's what I did. I dug to the bottom of the barrel and got the coldest one I could find. I was nervous, because she probably knew I wasn't legal, but she never asked me for my ID. The beer rang up for ninety-nine cents; I paid for it and practically ran to the car, hoping I wouldn't be seen. *Yea baby, Got em!*

Since the drive to the store only took me about five minutes then I knew I only had about five minutes to get back. This did not leave a lot of time to consume a quart of beer. I drove away from the store before I opened the beer.

The initial drink was a little bitter, which may have had something to do with the cost, but got better as I continued to drink. I tried to drink as much as possible and as quickly as possible because the clock was ticking. As hard as I tried, I didn't finish it, but surprisingly enough I got more than half down before I threw the remainder out the window. Initially, I felt okay. I really didn't know what to expect or how I should have felt after chugging a half quart of malt liquor for the first time. After I made it home I immediately went to the bathroom to brush my teeth and wash my face, trying to hide the smell of alcohol as much as I could. In the bathroom I began to feel a little strange; I had a dizzying feeling. It intensified so I had to let the lid down on the toilet to sit down and get myself together. "WTF is happening to me?" is what I was thinking and I was scared as hell.

The feeling that was now taking over was probably what it feels like to be drunk. As I made my way to my bedroom, all I could think about was I can't fall asleep this way. What if I don't wake up? Getting in bed was very scary because I was afraid to fall asleep drunk. I was scared because it all happened so quickly and I didn't feel good. I tried to stay awake, but I had no control over my slumber. I couldn't stop myself from going to sleep. I must have slept okay, because I don't remember having any bad dreams that night. I can honestly say that the advice from my friend worked! I just didn't like the way the beer made me feel. It was a while before I tried it again. Like the rest of the students, I would have to learn how to cope with my problems in a way that would work best for me. Drinking would not be it.

As I continued to float through high school feeling meaningless and without purpose, I would put up a good façade. Although I was smiling on the outside, I was carrying a lot of pain on the inside. I had no choice though, because I had no solutions.

On no day in particular, I was being my usual disruptive self in Mrs. Johnson's class and she was having no part of it. I can't forget this day because it was the day my life began to change. On this day I was acting a complete fool, being distractive, trying to get a laugh which was something I did quite often. The teacher, Mrs. Katherine Johnson, kindly walked over to my desk. Now I'm thinking here she goes again, "Go to the office", but not today. She bent over and said very softly, "Don't leave when the bell rings. See me after class". The class, of course, was "whoop-ing and aw-ing", because I got in trouble. When the bell rang, she slowly shuffled through some papers at her desk while waiting for every student to exit the classroom. Then she told me to come over to where she was standing in the corner of her class behind the door.

As I approached, her facial expression changed to a look of disgust and anger. Before she said what she had to say, she gave me a huge hug and said, "Keith Jenkins, you are "F"ing up badly! I watch you come to my class day in and day out and act a damn fool! You have the potential to do whatever you set your mind to! But you're "F"ing up!" In tears, she said, "You are one of the smartest students I've ever had the privilege to teach and I will not sit and watch you throw it away!" Now, I'm crying, she's crying. I didn't know what to say but as she continued to talk, she asked me, "What are your plans for the future?"

Still sniffing, I said, "I want to go to Jackson State to major in music and be a member of the Sonic Boom of the South marching band, but I can't because I'm in Special Ed." She asked me, "Do you know what it would take to accomplish that goal?"

"No ma'am." I said.

She said, "A lot of hard work, but you can do it. You have the potential and I know you can do it. I'm going to help you!" She gave me another hug and told me she loved me.

Leaving her class feeling optimistic although I was unsure of how this would play out because I didn't know if she had enough influence to make these things happen for me. I didn't know it only took a recommendation from my Special Education teacher to change my future. She could request an evaluation to have me tested out of Special Ed and into general studies.

With that, she quickly got the ball rolling. She called and scheduled a meeting with my parents to explain her recommendation and why she felt compelled to have me re-evaluated. Over the next couple of weeks, Mrs.

Johnson started preparing me for this evaluation. It was a three-hour test that I had to pass to exit out of the Special Education program. Everything she thought was on the test we reviewed. She pushed and pushed and pushed. As hard as I studied and as hard and I tried, there was still this thing called self-doubt that crept in to make me think I couldn't do this, telling me, *You're a failure. You're just not smart enough to get this done.* I was so nervous, almost to the point that I didn't want to take the test, but with her cheering me on I knew I wouldn't fail. I had to do this for both of us. This was going to be my ticket off this road to nowhere.

Test day was finally here. I had to quickly get past my emotions of the day, pushing out the self-doubt, because there was work to be done. It was a long test and somewhat difficult, but surprisingly enough, not as difficult as I thought it would be. Most of the credit though should have been given to Mrs. Johnson who had prepared me really well. The test administrator was gracious enough to allow the extra time that I needed so that I wouldn't have to rush through my responses. She wanted me to take my time and not worry about sections that I would potentially not complete. She knew I would make careless mistakes if I was in a rush. The test started around eight thirty and I finished after lunch. It was comprehensive and covered every subject. As I was handing my test to the administrator, she asked me, "Well, how did you do?"

With some hesitation, I said, "I guess okay."

A couple of weeks had passed before the results came back. The test administrator would normally give the results to the recommending teacher or counselor so they could contact the parents, but this time the administrator wanted to meet with my parents and Mrs. Johnson directly. Of course the first thing I thought was that bad news was coming. "Failed" was all I could hear in my head while the administrator was explaining the test measures and how it was graded. She explained that each section was worth a certain percentage; the children must be able to read and in their own words explain what they read. As she was going through her long winded explanations, I'm thinking lady, just get with it, *What did I make?* My heart was racing just waiting on her to say I didn't pass, but she turned and looked directly at my parents and said, "Mr. and Mrs. Jenkins, there was a mistake made by placing Keith in the program. Your son should have never been placed in Special Education. There are ways the district should have handled his behavior issues other than placing him in this program. Based on his scores he should not have been here." She turned and thanked Mrs. Johnson for making the recommendation and for noticing my potential. It was a day I will never forget; to hear someone say I didn't belong in Special Education was a feeling I can't explain.

As I began to make the transition into regular classes, one thing was for sure, I was scared. The fear did not end with leaving Special Ed. It actually intensified because I was now entering into a higher level of learning. As soon as I started my new classes, I immediately felt out of place. I felt like the new kid at a new school. I didn't realize how far behind I was until I was in class. Special Education crippled me. Whether I was supposed to be there or not, I was. I didn't learn a whole lot, probably due to no fault of my instructors, but I just didn't understand or take the time to try to understand what was being taught. When I started taking regular classes, I wasn't familiar with the material. I was behind in a lot of the subject matter so I had to learn and get caught up at the same time. I thought about failing more than succeeding and there were times when I had a mind to quit. But I kept telling myself, *Quit and do what? Return to Special Ed?* That was not an option especially with Mrs. Johnson by my side pushing me through.

Because I was much farther behind than the other students, I felt very intimidated and I could not keep up. While I was smart enough to test out of Special Education, I didn't feel I was smart enough to stay out. I thought for sure they would try to send me back and one thing about it, I was NOT going back. I had to buckle down and get after it. Mrs. Johnson made sure of that. She continued to help me. She would not accept any excuses because she felt excuses would only give me a reason to quit and not try. She would constantly remind me that the goals that we talked about required hard work. I couldn't fulfill those goals without it. She went even as far as to set up my schedule so I could have one class with her for tutoring. She continued to push me throughout the remainder of the school year.

By the time I got to twelfth grade my perspective of school had changed and it was not as much of a struggle to get up and go to class every day. It was primarily because I didn't have as many classes as before. My goal was to graduate with a regular diploma with hopes of going to college later. I didn't want the "Certificate of Completion" given to students who finished in the Special Education program. That was just not going to be good enough for me, and with that document, I would have no way of accomplishing my goals. As a way to aid me in the accomplishment of my goals, Mrs. Johnson encouraged me to read over the summer. She said, "Pick up a book, newspaper, or a magazine" and "Underline or circle words you can't pronounce or are unsure of". And I did just that. She knew I was not reading on the level I should be on. She said, "Whether it's for five minutes or five lines or five words, I don't care, you have to start somewhere." She had high expectations of me and I had high expectations of myself. There were things I had to get done in order to graduate.

While I had Mrs. Johnson as a constant cheerleader in my corner rooting me on, that was not the case with other faculty in the school. There was a stigma with students labeled as "problem children" and quite frankly there were those who didn't want me in their class. I don't know if it was the previous behavior issues, or the fact that I had previously been in "Special Ed" that would cause them to have to instruct on a level slower than the normal pace of class, but nevertheless they made it known that they didn't want me to be there. I'll never forget in one class the teacher was having a discussion on life after high school. Each student was given a chance to say something brief about going to college or their plans following high school. When it was my turn to speak, the teacher quickly interrupted before I could say anything and said, "Now a word from our special guest." Special as in Special Ed is what she meant. I guess she got the last laugh that day. I was hurt from those remarks but had to put on a good face. Some students laughed along with her, while others could see my pain. This same teacher told me that "College ain't for everybody." This was very discouraging. That wasn't something I wanted to hear. How is it that, the person who was supposed to build me up, was tearing me down. But not every teacher had that type of attitude towards me. Thank God for Mrs. Johnson and others like her.

In school I had many fears that resulted from the pressure brought on from thoughts of life after high school and my ability to succeed. I wasn't having the typical thoughts a graduating senior might have like what college should I attend? What should my major be? My fears were basic, but huge! There was something inside of me that I had been dealing with for a long time. My biggest fear was *FAILURE*.

Every senior was prepping for the state standardized test that each student had to pass in order to graduate. This was way before the days of "No child left behind", because it was evident there were many years I was left behind. There were no classes that were structured around standardized tests. In my day, you took classes to learn and were left to take the comprehensive test at the end of the year in order to graduate. If you passed, you graduated, if you failed, you didn't. This was another hurdle I had to jump, but I was assured that with hard work, I would pass.

No students were given special treatments during the test. I appreciated this because I was able to focus on the test instead of focusing on being treated like a Special Ed Student. I wanted to earn my passing mark just like every other student in that room. I had goals set and I was on track to graduate and earn a regular diploma. While I had some hope of possibly passing, I still had that high level of fear and self-doubt in the back of my mind.

Mrs. Johnson an ever present fixture during my high school career was still helping me; she made me study more and she would always say I had to work harder to get it. Getting it was up to me. Along with all of my other class work, I had to work extra hard to maintain what I had accomplished as well as study for this test. Preparing for the test was not easy. There were long nights of study and lots of senior social time I had to give up. But with the support of my parents along with help from Mrs. Johnson, I took the test and was able to pass it. This was a great feeling; to know I could pass a test that all regular students had to take. For the first time in a really long time I felt normal, like all the others. I was shocked and elated to hear that not only did I pass it, but I actually did better than some of the other seniors that had taken the test. Because of this, I was getting closer and closer to accomplishing my goals. I felt like my dreams of going to college were going to come sooner vs later. It was a much-needed boost in my confidence.

I was able to maintain my grades at a passing level throughout my senior year. My behavior had gotten a lot better but near the end of the school year my bad dreams began to start back. I tried really hard to ignore them but couldn't. I finally decided to share them with Kenny. He was the only person in my family that I had ever mentioned my dreams to. I struggled with the decision because while I wanted to share so he could feel my pain and my fear, I didn't want him to think I was crazy. I knew how I sounded though, and I was having a really hard time trying to explain them to myself so it was going to be even more difficult to get anyone to understand what I was experiencing. It had always been easier just to deal with it alone. I told Kenny "I feel like something is always surrounding me, in my space, trying to get at me. I can be standing around talking and out of nowhere these images just appear. Today they may be small, and tomorrow, they are larger than they were the day before. They look like they're growing. They're scary and they haunt me. As a child I couldn't rest because they would taunt me in my sleep which is why I was so tired in school. That's why I was always sleeping in class and fell behind. Then the kids would just make fun of me which is why I started acting up. It was really a distraction. I can't really explain it and I can't explain why I'm so angry all the time. It's like I'm mad at the world and it's done nothing to me. I want to talk to momma and dad about it, but I know they'll just think I'm crazy. I'm not really sure if you even believe me right now. That's why I've just always kept it to myself."

Since I was in the mood to share, I also opened up about how embarrassed I was about being in Special Ed. I told him how angry I would get sitting in a Special Ed math class with the teacher using Popsicle sticks as a tool to count! "Hell, why was I in this class". "That's why when you walked by her class I was sitting in the hall because I told her there are no Popsicle sticks in the real world. That's when she put me out." I told him I would be so embarrassed that when Mrs. Johnson would open the door to the classroom, I run to the back and hide because I didn't want anyone to know I was in that class. Especially because I knew I was smarter than that and I should have never been in there to begin with. I told him my behavior should have never dictated the level I was being taught on.

My behavior should have determined the environment but not the level. We talked about some of the other stuff I was going through since I left Special Ed and how I was being mistreated by some teachers. There are those who were put in a position to work with "problem children", but chose not to help them. They should be pushing the child in the areas where they show potential. You're no good to them if you're just shutting them down. Special Ed was a problem because you had tenth, eleventh and twelfth graders in the same class, all doing the same work. This was my problem. Then I wasn't being taught to excel, I was only being taught to function! If they could evaluate me and could tell my parents I've got a problem, why not evaluate me to understand my potential?

I was determined to go to college and to prove to myself that I could. But there were questions in the back of my mind. Am I smart enough? Was I equipped for college? While these were concerns, to be honest, they were not at the forefront of my mind because I had my heart set on marching in the band; that's what gave me hope. I had dreams of making it to the next level and found comfort as well as hope in being able to foster that dream.

As the final weeks of school approached, I worked extremely hard to make sure everything I needed to graduate was taken care of. The day I stopped by my councilor's office to see if I was going to, she had a smile on her face when she gave me the news, "Well, Keith, looks like you did it. You will graduate! You have completed all of the required courses and received all the credits needed to graduate with a regular diploma." I could not believe it. I could but I couldn't. With the struggles I've had, to finally hear this news was awesome. The counselor cried with me as she gave me the news I was graduating. To know I had successfully accomplished something I put my mind to doing was the greatest feeling. Over the last couple of days of school, I talked to Mrs. Johnson and thanked her for all she had done for me. I told her, had she not taken the time to invest in me, I wouldn't be in the position I was in. I asked her if she thought I would make it in college. She said, "Keith, you have the potential to do whatever you set your mind on doing. Yes, I believe you can do it!"

With graduation nearing, and all boxes checked, the constant cloud over me was always, I was not where I should be. I knew I was academically behind because I had missed a lot of work. It became evident to me when I looked at Kenny's books and the materials he was working on and what I was working on. There was no comparison. They were worlds apart. He'd try to explain the work, but I didn't understand it. Deep down in my heart, I was grateful to be graduating but if the truth be told I still felt inferior in comparison.

The night of graduation, I had to pull it together. I had no reason to feel down about anything; it was one of the happiest nights of my life. Or at least it should have been, but for whatever reason I felt down. As the graduating class was lining up, I assumed every student was excited about this special moment. Some were even crying. As for me, I had no tears. I was happy but fighting not to be sad. I didn't want to feel out of place because I had worked hard to be in the position I was in. Although I had the feeling that some of my classmates and teachers thought I shouldn't be getting the diploma that was being handed to me.

PART II

GROWING UP

Choices can determine what road you will travel. It's a large part of growing up and if you choose poorly you may suffer the consequences of those actions. You just hope and pray that you will be able to live beyond those actions. You should learn as much as possible from the failures of others and save yourself some headaches.

-Keith D. Jenkins

GROWING UP

FAILURE

ONE OF THE things I loved most about growing up was that my parents weren't strict. We had the freedom to be boys. This meant we could run, play, and experience the things that boys were supposed to experience without the extra precautions because you were nervous about what your child might be doing. Now they didn't give us free range to just run the streets. They had rules that we had to follow and were enforced if we got out of hand. And that was the one thing you didn't want to experience was Mack Jenkins' enforcement of the rules. So, for the most part, we tried to abide. These rules were set in place as a guideline for my brothers and me to follow and all in all, I would say we did. The older we got, the more freedoms we were given. Now, I could come and go as I pleased, with a few restrictions. But even with restrictions, freedom was something I really enjoyed. I guess it made me feel more like an adult. I felt they trusted me to make the right decisions. I knew I didn't need them looking over my shoulders. They had raised me and my brothers right, given us what we needed to make good decisions, and that's what I had planned to do. Show them I could handle this responsibility.

What I quickly found out was, new found freedom was good, but in certain areas, I didn't need it and couldn't handle it. Mentally I wasn't ready for a lot of the things I encountered entering college and one thing I knew for sure, Mrs. Johnson was not going with me to help me along the way. There would be no hand holding when it came to registering for school, touring the campus, setting up classes, and talking with the folks at financial aid. It was quite overwhelming. I guess this was probably what was meant at the time when the statement was made to me that "College ain't for everybody". Dealing with these things had me settling back into my old mindset. The self-doubt was coming back, but truthfully told, I'm not so sure that it really left. Maybe it was just put on pause for a while. My confidence level was shrinking again. I was still struggling to overcome my past, fighting to stay ahead of current problems, all while trying to embrace new beginnings. I was torn.

I felt I was cautious with everything I did because I no longer had help from teachers to make decisions; it was all on me. But not cautious in the sense of one traveling through a yellow light not wanting to get caught on red by the police, more like choosing to not walk through that door because you don't know what lies on the other side of it. I guess in my mind FAILURE stood on the other side of the door. I was still struggling with this 'I won't succeed' mentality. I know I had to make my own choices and accept responsibility for my decisions, but I thought about failure more than I thought about being successful. I never considered my potential to be or do great things. While others embraced the 'failure is not an option' mentality, I was still struggling with basic decisions. The challenge was not the ability to do everything myself, it was doing it correctly. It's basically because I didn't have a plan. What I've grown to learn is that every dream must be accompanied with a plan to implement it. Good or bad, I had them– dreams. The problem I faced was that I didn't know how to put my dreams into actions because I didn't know how to plan for anything. I was struggling with how to work through the next chapter of my life. *What now? What next? School and what?* Mentally, I failed at everything because I felt there was no way I could accomplish what I needed to accomplish. New things scared me and what I didn't understand overwhelmed me, so much so, that I stopped trying.

THE BOOM

I T FINALLY CAME, my acceptance letter from Jackson State University for the upcoming school year. I was one step closer to becoming a member of the Sonic Boom of the South marching band. I was going to be a *Tubadog*. I still didn't believe it was possible. You would have thought that this would have encouraged me, but it didn't. I guess I just wasn't mature enough to encourage myself out of the state I was in. Yes, the band was my ticket into college and had even provided a little financial aid to attend, but kids don't go to college just to play in a band. That's not the primary reason for going to college. I think back to what my dad had said "You just want to go play that damn horn" and maybe he was right. Maybe that was my whole reason for being there. It was what I was comfortable with because it was what I knew how to do. Eventually, this whole education thing was going to come up and then my secret would be told. The baggage would follow me and everyone at Jackson State would know I was a fraud. I shouldn't be here nor should I have a diploma. I had struggled so much with education. I felt there was no reason to get excited. All of these emotions came rushing back to the surface mainly because I had learning difficulties and I did not believe in my abilities to be successful in college. I felt I would be exposed. Despite all the negative thoughts, I still managed to prepare myself for what would hopefully be the start of a dream come true.

After successfully auditioning, I was invited back to a two-week band camp on the campus of Jackson State. I felt proud leaving home because I was working towards my goals. This was one of the few things that I had done all by myself and felt very accomplished because of it. Also, the support of my parents and family was amazing. I was surrounded by love, encouragement, and of course covered by their prayers.

Checking into band camp and seeing other kids being dropped off while others drove themselves to camp were special moments to experience. I didn't feel out of place because I was surrounded by others who, like me, shared the same love for music. I did however feel intimidated by the new surroundings, because I didn't know what was next or what to expect. But like them, I was in for the ride.

All the new members were required to attend the meet and greet on the first night of band camp. This was a time to mingle with each other as well as to scare the crap out of the new kids on the block. Getting use to the large crowd was an adjustment for me. My emotions were all over the place. My nerves finally settled after a while. Let's face it, most of the newbies or "crabs" as they liked to call us, were probably as nervous and scared as I was. Everyone was just trying to put on a good face and trying not to look like *that kid*.

After a few introductions of the staff, the director got up to speak. In his opening he said, "Not all of you are going to make it, so look around and see who you won't see at the end of these two weeks." He was looking directly at me as he was making the statement. Never would I have imagined that failure was a possibility in The Boom. I was going to do everything in my being to ensure that I didn't fail. For the next two weeks I went through band camp feeling pressured and anxious in fear that I wouldn't get over this hurdle. And a hurdle indeed it was. Camp was no picnic.

I was prepared as best I could have been for the musical challenge, but getting up at five every morning for physical training (PT) was a whole new challenge. It felt like sixty percent of the day was PT with little to no time for anything else in between; days at camp didn't end until one in the morning. Those were some long days. During this time I found that even eating was over-rated. There were times during camp I skipped meals just to get some sleep. There wasn't a lot of time to do both. I must admit all this physical activity did come with its benefits. Before entering camp I weighed close to three hundred pounds. Because of the strenuous days and missed meals, I could tell I had begun to lose weight. I don't know how much I lost but I was looking and feeling better. My shrinking waistline was definitely increasing my confidence and ego. Socially I was coming out of my shell. I'd gotten better at interacting with others and because of the weight loss I no longer felt socially inept. Meanwhile, camp occupied the entire day with rehearsal after rehearsal coupled with physical training in the morning, noon and evening.

It was not uncommon for "old heads" to come and check out the newbies during band camp. During the first night of camp an older gentleman who was a past member of the band came back to talk to several of the new members including me. I knew him because he had attended high school with my older brothers. Because I knew him I was very interested in what he had to say. "You guys are going to be introduced to some new things, some good and some bad. But if you know right from wrong, you'll do well. I hate to say it, but some of y'all are going to get caught up with experimenting. If you don't do it now, don't start it and don't try it." What he said next seemed as if I was the only one in the room. "Some of y'all drink and some of y'all don't." *Was I transparent? Could he see through me? Did he know I had already experimented?* I wasn't like most students who would be first introduced to alcohol in college. I already had, but how did he know this? Turning to me, he said, "And you know you don't need to drink nothing 'cause your dad and brother were both alcoholics." I don't know if he was trying to get a laugh, but he got one from some of my classmates. *But what could I say? Hell, it was the truth.*

At the time, I didn't feel there was anything wrong with the advice he was giving, and I didn't feel like I'd disregarded his plea. At the time I believed I was responsible enough to drink. I guess I really didn't think the message was for me specifically, because I didn't think I would be the one to get caught up. I had my taste in high school. Although it helped me deal with the voices and the images, it wasn't anything I was particularly fond of. Outside of that benefit, I could live without it.

CLASS

I STARTED OUT on a high and very excited about class eagerly wanting to learn and see what higher education had in store. I wanted to prove this is what I was here for, to get an education and not just play a horn. I quickly came to discover that higher education was serious business. Even at the introductory level my classes were overwhelming and very intimidating. It was the same story all over again, just a different day.

Sitting in class I felt like I was in a foreign country listening to an instructor speak in a language I couldn't interpret. There were a number of things I was unfamiliar with. I couldn't say if the material was hard or not because I just didn't understand what was being taught. I remember thinking this is not going to be easy, as I was trying to decipher what my college algebra instructor had said. Math was never my strongest subject, but having a teacher trying to be cool, coupled with a language barrier, and a student who was already behind, was just not a formula for success.

This took me back to the memories of my high school teacher who said "College ain't for everybody" because clearly I was in over my head. I was not prepared for college, yet I had the desire to be educated. It was becoming

34

my reality that I was going to have to accept that anyone that struggles with illiteracy has no place in college.

The other missing link for me was Mrs. Johnson. I didn't have the support system that I had in high school. I didn't have the teacher that was going to invest in me to ensure that I didn't fail and push me to succeed. I didn't feel comfortable enough to go to my instructors and ask for help. I didn't have a clue as to what they were teaching and I didn't try to seek out help from any of my classmates. There were study groups available and I'm sure I could have gone to other students, but I felt like the things I was struggling with I should have already known. I knew I would be judged if I went to anyone else and asked for help. I was supposed to know this stuff because I had made it to college. I was too humiliated to ask someone for help so yet again, I found myself struggling to get by in school. The more things changed, the more they stayed the same.

ADDICTION

MY FIRST OFFICIAL college drink happened one night at an off campus event. It was what I like to call a "get together". Nothing fancy, just some senior band members having a house party with a few of my crab brothers scattered about. When I walked in, I saw what I would expect to see at your typical house party. There were folks at the table talking noise and playing spades, a dominoes game over in the corner, some loud music in the background, and plenty to drink. Now this wasn't the high quality, top shelf stuff because we were college students, but it was a little better than the quart that I had during my first experience. I really don't remember what I chose to drink. It was insignificant at the time. I had the drink and at first everything was okay. I continued to mingle with friends but after a while I noticed an unusual feeling. I felt a shift as if something had entered my body. Not wanting to seem weird or appear drunk, I didn't mention it and tried to ignore it as best I could. After that night I had no desire to drink for a while. I wasn't bothered by any bad dreams at the moment so I didn't need to. These days, I was feeling relatively normal.

I was really starting to enjoy my college experience, that is, outside of class. I was still struggling in that area. Hanging out on the yard was great. I was meeting new people, becoming a little more popular with the ladies, building some strong bonds with a few of the fellows, and overall just having a great time. The freedom was awesome especially because I had no curfew.

One night following a pep rally, some of the band members and and I got together at an off campus location to hang out. There was alcohol present but I didn't feel the need or pressure to drink. I didn't want to look like the odd man out so I grabbed a beer and continued to mingle. I noticed that beer was becoming my go-to drink and I was developing a strange craving for the taste of it. As I was starting to enjoy several of them, my desire to drink intensified and all of a sudden I couldn't explain what was happening. All I know is, what I was feeling didn't feel right. Is this what being drunk felt like? This was a scary feeling initially. It finally mellowed out as the night went on but I knew something wasn't right. I had a tingling in my body and after a while I decided to just go home.

My drive home was scary because this was the first time I'd driven a car knowing I had been drinking more than I should have. I didn't think I was under the influence, but I definitely had a buzz. I turned off the radio and let the windows down so that I would stay alert. As I got off the highway and began to merge onto the off ramp, I saw the image from my childhood dreams. I did a double-take to make sure I was seeing correctly. Turning left, I saw the image running in the same direction I was traveling in. It was pointing and waving as if it was trying to flag me down. *Was I going crazy? Was this the alcohol?* I tried to shake it off and convince myself that I didn't just see that. It was either the alcohol or I was losing my mind.

I tried to erase the thought and put it out of my mind but I knew exactly what I had seen.

This was the night before the first home game, and I was terrified and excited all at the same time. To keep my mind from dwelling on what had just happened I tried to do little mundane tasks around the house. I got my band uniform ready and made sure my shoes were polished. I was really just hoping to get some sleep this night without having any bad dreams, but little did I know as I drifted to sleep they awaited me.

The sounds of the dream started very soft and faint but as the sounds grew, they became unbearable. It was as if there were a million voices speaking at the same time, each voice uttering something different. As the images appeared, I began to sweat profusely. Amongst a crowd of images, a smaller demon appeared; the one from my childhood dreams. As I remembered, it was dark as night with those scary eyes. Then all the images spoke at the same time and together they said, "Master!" The cries in the background intensified as they spoke. Next, the larger demon appeared. It was standing in front of me with his back turned towards me. As it began to turn around there were flames bursting from his eyes. Sweating, crying, and scared, I tried to turn my head in an effort not to look at it, but I couldn't.

It spoke and said, "It's okay. You can look at me; I'm not like him."

I did everything I could to move but couldn't.

It said, "Allow me to introduce myself; I AM SATAN! You've heard of me. You refer to me as this thing, a demon in your dreams. The smaller demons' job is to do as I command!"

I remember feeling like I was in some type of restraint not able to move. I remember crying out, "LORD, PLEASE HELP ME!"

He laughed and said, "Funny, don't you know prayer doesn't work down here?"

I said, "My grandmother said the name Jesus works anywhere! Just speak it."

Satan's reply was, "Only if you believe what you're saying."

Then I asked, "Why me?"

His reply was, "Well, it goes back to when you were a small child and your great-grandfather held you in his arms and prophesied over you saying, God was going to do amazing things in your life and that you would be favored by

Him. Anyone favored by God poses a potential threat to me and my kingdom and my plans are to prevent that from happening."

Trembling, I said, "You don't have to worry about me. Why am I here? Why am I here?" I woke up confused and terrified. I didn't quite understand the dream. I just knew there was a hold over my life but didn't know why. This was the last time I dreamed of Satan and his demons.

My life spiraled out of control after this. I went from being a social drinker to needing a drink to get up in the morning. After starting my day with my morning cup of Joe, preferably beer, I would go to campus. Although I was on the 'yard', I wasn't going to class much. I was mostly hanging out because I had become totally dependent on alcohol. It made my life a living hell, and yet I felt there was nothing I could do about it. I had quickly become consumed by the addiction and *I was now living the dream*; the one that I couldn't explain.

The more I drank, the more I began to have cravings, usually at awkward times of the day. What started as social drinking quickly developed into a dependency. There were times I would drink before class or in the middle of the day and for no apparent reason. When I realized I had a drinking problem, I kept it to myself instead of reaching out for help. I dealt with it the same way I had handled everything else–alone. I didn't want anyone feeling sorry for me and I certainly didn't want to be a burden to others.

For a long time I lived with a condition that I couldn't explain. It was a condition that affected most of my childhood. Living in constant fear all of those years became normal to me. Drinking helped me by providing a way to escape those fears. I knew that I was scared of being alone because most times even in the company of others, I still felt lonely.

Drinking became more than just a means to cope; it became my company keeper. It helped me deal with a lot of the uncertainties I had experienced. I tried to manage it, thinking it was something I could control and overcome. I knew the effects drinking had on others because I had seen it firsthand, mainly with my dad. Were there possible warning signs that I had missed in my life or things said that maybe I didn't hear? Not wanting to embrace this obvious fact, I had to come to grips with the fact that I was an alcoholic!

Most of my life now revolved around drinking. Initially hiding my addiction was easy. I tried to stay sociable, interacting with friends and family, but if you come to enough social functions drunk, people start to notice. Soon enough, it became apparent to others that I had a problem. As far as class was concerned, I was only taking introductory level courses which were too hard because I was still playing catchup from high school. It was a challenge to just to keep up. I didn't understand a lot of what was being taught and the drinking didn't help either. I felt I was in way over my head. For me school had become something to pass time. I was never going to walk away with a degree. School was just a social setting centered on football season, hanging out, and parties. The more parties I attended, the more I drank.

My mother gave me an allowance while I was in school. There was no splurging though. It was supposed to be enough money to keep me afloat during the week. The funds were for basic necessities like food, gas, and books. It was a sacrifice for her to even give me a few dollars, and how did I repay her? I used the money to support my habit. I'd take it and put half in the gas tank and spend the other half on beer. When mom found out I was misusing my allowance, she cut me off. I was left with no other choice but to support myself financially. That's when I turned to selling drugs to support my addiction. Thankfully this career choice was very short-lived.

I had become a drifter over the past four years focused on two things, drinking and the band. By now I had given up on any chance of finishing school. It was the final week of the football season, and for some band members, the final game. It was a week I could barely remember. The one thing that gave my life meaning and purpose was centered on this marching band. It was my reason for getting out of the bed every morning. For most students it was the end of an era but for me it felt like the end of my life. There were others who had goals and they were close to accomplishing them. I had no idea what was next for me. I kept asking myself, "What am I going to do now?" It was more bitter than sweet. This was supposed to be the time when you graduate and move on to the next chapter in life, but I was stuck doing nothing, living for the moment.

The Friday before the final game of the season was like a band family reunion. It was tradition for alumni from all over the country to gather for this event. On the practice field that Friday night, I was so drunk that I was asked to stand on the sideline and watch. I was in a daze the entire night. I walked around mingling with other alumni trying to act as normal as possible but inside I was dying. On Saturday morning, early the next day, we had practice, but I don't know how I got there. I was so out of it still hungover from the night before, I was of no use to anyone. One of the band directors put me in his car to sober up and I slept until he woke me up hours later. I went home but instead of sleeping it off, I was back at it again. I drank back-to-back all day long. We had to report to campus again at five that evening to prepare for the game, load up the buses, and head to the stadium. A couple of the members said some pretty harsh things to me, but I was in no shape to respond. Had they known what had given my life purpose over the last four years was now coming to an end, they probably wouldn't have said the things they said. But maybe they needed to be said. It was one of my lowest moments. I didn't feel suicidal, however, at that moment not marching in the band anymore felt like death because I didn't have anything else after this. With the football season over, the one thing that had given me purpose was now coming to an end.

I embarrassed the entire program marching into the stadium that night. There were a series of unfortunate events that transpired over a short amount of time. Someone had to pull me out of bushes that I don't remember falling into. The pregame performance for this game was dedicated to those members who were performing their final game. Looking into the stands filled with thousands of fans, I remember singing very loudly and off-key, "It's so hard to say goodbye to yesterday." I don't think I played a single note the entire game. It was routine that eight minutes before halftime the band would exit the stands to get ready for the halftime performance. I remember taking one step and falling into the concrete stands; I was literally passed out at the game in front of a crowd of thousands. I was a disaster. The young lady I was dating at that time, embarrassed as she was, came to see about me and did what she could to help me. Since she couldn't handle me, she called my mother and Kenny and they came and took me home.

I must have slept at least a day because when I got up my mother was in the kitchen cooking Sunday dinner and she asked me if I was okay. I'd been too drunk to be embarrassed and little did anyone know I was dying from this disease.

This was it, the end was here. After the band there was nothing left. After High School I had a next step, but now I didn't. I didn't have a plan, I didn't have a solution. Again, I was floating.

QUITTING

T HERE WERE A number of things that should have motivated me to quit, the first being my dad. His death was from illnesses related to his abuse of alcohol. I was at work when I got the call that he was being rushed to the hospital. I couldn't handle the news so I did what I do best–I got drunk. Initially, I was too drunk to make it to the hospital and I was definitely in no condition to be around my family. After I finally sobered up I went to see him. It was heartbreaking. He had a massive seizure and the doctors said they didn't believe he would pull through. He was lying there full of wires and tubes, hooked up to more monitors than you can imagine. I felt like I was looking at the man in the mirror. Not because I was the spitting image of my dad, but because this would be my future if I didn't get myself together. I could just hear folks saying now "The apple doesn't fall far from the tree." I was under this generational curse. I was really seeing myself for the first time. My dad's drink of choice was now mouthwash because nothing else would do. It basically ate up his internal organs and what he would ultimately succumb to. The night he died, I remember standing by his bedside having a brief conversation with a young nurse about his condition. Everything beyond that was a blur. I drank heavily most of the next week. I vaguely remember the funeral and some of the family events that went on. This should have done one of two things, motivate me to get better, or cause me to become worse.

My children should have motivated me to quit as well, but they didn't. I wanted to build a relationship with them, but I wanted the bottle more. My three older children were born during my college years. I honestly tried to make the best decisions when it came to them, but I won't lie and say I was always on the right side of right. If I had a reason for not being what I should have been to my children, drinking was it. My addiction to alcohol pulled me in ways I never could imagine. I was what society would label as a deadbeat dad.

As a result of my addiction, I purposely stayed out of their lives because I felt I had nothing to offer them. If I had to be honest with myself, the mothers didn't want me involved anyway. I was excluded from each of their births but I couldn't get angry at them for making this decision. I'm sure they felt excluding me was the right thing to do at the time.

Society looks down on men like me. People tend to be critical and don't completely understand the cause of a father's absence. I was a man with three kids by three different women and no stable employment. This bothered me because I wasn't a sorry man–just a man that wanted to be involved but wasn't in a position to do so. Since people really didn't know this about me, "sorry man" was the best thing they could call me. I had to defend my addiction because there were times when I had to choose between supporting my children or my addiction. I was called out because folks said that if I can support my drinking habits, then I could support my children. I never disagreed with what was said but the problem was I wasn't just casually drinking for leisure or pleasure. I had an addiction and when a choice has to be made, addiction almost always wins. At this stage in my life, it did. Since I couldn't support them financially, I thought it was best to stay away. I know this created a problem for their mothers having to deal with this alone. It was unfair to them to have to bear this burden and deal with all the financial woes brought on by my absence. I was truly sorry for this, but at the time, I was incapable of admitting it to myself and I definitely didn't have the capacity to apologize to them either.

For a long time I didn't tell folks I had kids, not because I was embarrassed by them, but more that I was embarrassed by what I wasn't doing, for or with them. I never liked to hear guys brag on how they didn't have to pay any child support or about how little they had to pay. But I couldn't judge, because even with the little support they were bragging about, they were probably more invested both financially and emotionally than I had been.

I was depressed and I felt undeserving of the right to be active in their lives. During the few times when I would get my oldest daughter I would be extremely proud. It was in those moments that I wouldn't drink. Her spirit was so precious. *How could she have a father this bad? How could I fully love her, when I didn't love myself?* The drinking was destroying everything about me and there was nothing I could do about it. I only wanted the best for my children and right now I was unable to give them my best. The rejection towards my children wasn't all about me. I simply didn't want them to have to grow up being associated with an alcoholic father. In my mind I was only trying to protect them from the disappointment and embarrassment of what would later come. They needed a stable father, not a drunk daddy which is all I could offer them. I was trying to measure up to someone I couldn't be.

So yes, I had more than enough reasons to quit. I had generational curses that needed to be torn down, I had children that needed a father, but I just didn't have the capacity to stop. People would ask me "Why won't you stop?" To be honest, I had no reason to stop because drinking was working for me and people failed to realize that quitting wasn't easy. It was like an abusive relationship that I knew was unhealthy and turbulent, but kept going back to, because I was "in love", so much so that I was willing to accept the abuse. However, there comes a time in your life when you have to acknowledge your problems and I was just about there. I knew I had a problem and I truly had a desire to get rid of it, but I wasn't exactly sure of how to go about it. I don't know when I first felt the desire to want to quit, but it had gotten to the point I would stay in bed because I didn't want to drink. I just couldn't stop. I knew if I stopped, it would potentially mean I would have to deal with some stuff that was being suppressed by the drinking. Drinking filled a lot of voids which is why I cherished the addiction so much. It provided a covering over many of the problems that had been hidden that I experienced as a child. These problems had become buried inside of me. Whether I had truly dealt with the problems or not, drinking gave me piece of mind. Unfortunately, what I thought was providing me with peace of mind had ultimately became the source of all my pain.

MY FIRST LOVE

DURING THIS PERIOD nothing was really working for me. School was a failure; I didn't have a stable relationship, and I was not involved in my children's lives. Drinking was all I had. My thirst for alcohol had become a morning, noon, and nightly habit. The thing about addiction is that it is not uncommon for one abuse to lead to another. For instance someone on cocaine might need to chase it with heroin to maintain the same level of high after repeated use. For me, I chased alcohol with sex. The more I drank the more sex I wanted. I didn't particularly make the best choices in women and were mostly using them for self-gratification. Sometimes I dealt with women who had low self-esteem, ones that I could easily manipulate in exchange for sex and beer. This was very selfish and reckless of me to allow these women to support me. Playing on the emotions of the vulnerable to get something in return was very dangerous on my part. It was not about building relationships, but about satisfying my thirst and my libido.

Although a few of the women I was manipulating developed feelings for me, alcohol was my girlfriend. She provided comfort to me when I was lonely, she provided me with confidence when I was down, she made me feel more desirable when I felt inadequate, and on the really good days she even argued with me. That was the type of relationship we had. One night I remember getting so drunk I began to argue with a twenty-four ounce can of beer. I said to it, "B@#!%, you don't give a damn about me." She responded, "I'm sorry, baby. I'll do better. Please don't put me down." One thing we knew how to do was make-up. I felt like it was some kind of spirit I was arguing with, not the alcohol itself but the driving force behind the abuse. One of the things I loved most about the relationship was that it gave me the ability to say whatever I wanted to with no regard. Of all of the years of verbal abuse I had endured, this relationship gave me the ability to release it. I didn't care what I said or who I said it to. Why was it so important to me to continue with this abusive, degrading, disrespectful relationship? Because it gave me purpose and I needed it to help me feel like I was somebody. With nowhere to go and no one to turn to, this relationship was my lifeline. It gave me what I needed to survive. What I didn't realize was that my world was in for a major disruption.

PART III

MY GIFT

The saying goes God gives you exactly what you need when you need it. Sometimes you just need something that will take your attention from your current situation even if only for a brief moment. Just a glance at something positive can be enough motivation to help inspire a person to change. It doesn't always come as you would have designed it, but once you realize it's a gift from him, you know that it was given to you for your good and for his glory.

-Keith D. Jenkins

THINGS REMEMBERED

I WAS NOW at a time in my life where things were okay, at least by my definition. They were okay because I was no longer drowning just staying afloat, but currently, that was fine with me. I was comfortable and accepted the fact that I had no aspirations. I was going nowhere fast. Work was the only thing really consuming my time and my life, outside of drinking. It wasn't the best of jobs, but it was enough to pay a few bills, and buy beer when I got off, which was essentially all I needed. I was still home with mom, so I didn't need much. I wasn't involved in any stable relationships although I was hanging out with a few women here and there. I wasn't investing any real time in my children only seeing the ones that were local when I could. Occasionally I would hang out because I was still relatively young and social, but again, I was that lonely man in a crowded room, just me and my bottle, watching and waiting. I wasn't really sure what I was waiting on at the time, I guess something breakthrough to happen. I can honestly say I was at peace with the lifestyle I was living. This was it; there were no expectations. I was settling for being an alcoholic. Even though I had become complacent I felt this was a better life for me because I didn't have to deal with the stresses of school and house, of real bills and growing up. Previously I'd had the desire to want more and experience new things, but that was not my current state of mind.

I struggled daily with this addiction and everyday it seemed as if life with it got harder and harder. There was no such thing as one day being better than the next. I couldn't ignore what the addiction had done to my appearance. Alcohol has a way of taking years from you which eventually shows up in the mirror. The more I drank, the more it aged me. I was not saying that I was all of that, but I am confident that I looked better before the addiction. The addiction made me ugly because I had an ugly problem. It was reflected in the way I looked and the way I lived. I had begun to look more like an alcoholic with each passing day and I couldn't find anything about myself that I would say I was pleased with. I was in a rut and it was easy to stay there because the depression that came along with the addiction was a familiar place for me.

On the morning of Christmas Eve I was coming off a typical night of drinking where I had drank a few beers and a couple of 'Walk Me Downs'. I was in bed still hungover when my phone rang. It was my homeboy wanting to go to the mall to get his parents a Christmas gift. He wouldn't take 'no' for an answer, adamantly insisting that I go to the mall with him. Apparently being rude wasn't working. This was the last thing I wanted to do since I was hungover. Little did I know a life-changing experience would be on the other side of this conversation.

I had no interest in going to the mall. He had a reason to go shopping; I didn't. He said, "Big Jinx, roll with yo boy to the mall."

I said, "Man, I'm still in bed, Go ahead without me, but get at me later."

He said, "I'll be there in twenty minutes." Apparently he didn't hear me say that I was in bed or he was just ignoring me altogether. "See you in twenty, Jinx," was all he said.

When he showed up he had coffee in hand, so I went back in the house to get my cup of Joe, beer in hand, got in the car, and off we went.

On the way to the mall we talked, and I told him I was tired of the women I was dealing with. I was ready to make a change. Although I knew I should not have been blaming the failures of my former relationships on skin complexions, I told him that I was done with light-skinned women. That was the type of women I had been physically attracted to, but it was not working out for me. I made the decision then and there I was going to start looking for me a chocolate girl. I'm sure this had nothing to do with nothing, but it's where I was at the time.

Why he chose Christmas Eve of all days to go looking for a Christmas gift is beyond me, but what else did I have to do that day? The holidays were pretty uneventful for me and outside of wishing my mom a Happy Birthday later that afternoon, I had nothing else to do that day. We perused a few stores and finally wandered upon a gift shop that didn't look too busy. In a corner of the store was a customer being helped by a young lady who immediately caught my eye. She was very attractive. I stayed my distance, trying not to stare but it was almost impossible not to look at her. She was the kind of woman any man would want to get with. My friend was on the other side of the store being helped by another young lady. So I just stood there staring at this young lady who'd so deeply caught my attention, trying my best not to be so obvious but she was just beautiful.

I stayed out of the way while she helped a customer, but I noticed that she seemed a bit down. It seemed as if she was only at work physically but mentally she seemed drained and very distant. I watched the customer laugh and joke with her and occasionally she'd laugh back but nothing more than just being nice. She really wasn't paying him, and certainly not me, any attention. Her looks were intimidating and I personally felt she was out of range for me. Besides there was no way a woman this beautiful was single.

After consulting with the other young lady in the store, my friend finally decided to have a doorknocker engraved for his parents' home. She told us it would be about four hours until our gift was ready so we would need to come back. I didn't want to walk the mall for another four hours but we told her we would be back. We came back after an hour in hopes that it would be ready and of course it wasn't. The young lady I had been staring at politely told us, "I told you guys four hours, it's only been an hour", "Please come back", "We're busy". After some time, maybe another half hour or so we came back again. This was really my opportunity to get another glimpse of her even though I was ready to leave the mall. There was nothing else there that was of interest to me. Finally her friend said "Since you guys won't leave us alone until we engrave this thing, we'll go ahead and move you to the front of the line." Just give us twenty minutes and then come back. We left the store and came back a few minutes later to pick up his order.

My boy was with the other young lady at the register laughing while she was wrapping up his order. My young lady was coming up to the front of the store from the back storage room. She seemed sad so I stayed my distance. I guess I was just watching and waiting. She was breathtaking and had a great figure. She was short and a little thick but that's how I liked my women. And the icing on the cake was that she was dark-skinned; just what the doctor had ordered. She stopped to get some merchandise out of a drawer and all I could think was *Claud have Mercy*. She was bent over and I was in the perfect spot to get a good look at her assets. She stayed bent over for a good little minute which was long enough for me to build up the courage to make my move.

My boy had begun asking her some random questions when she made it to the register, you know the typical stuff, "What's your name?", "Are you married?", "Do you have a man?" basically finding out all I needed to know. I was feeling like a dirty buddy, because I wasn't sure if my friend was interested as well, but thank you for clearing the way. Since I didn't see any numbers exchange, she was fair game. It was time for me to seize the moment.

I said 'hello' and the way she spoke back was definitely different. We talked a minute and instantly I felt something different about her. She had a face of innocence. I think it was her smile and the dimples that won me over. She was definitely not what I was used to. As we got ready to leave the store, I took a chance, gave her my number, and asked her to give me a call whenever her time allowed.

Leaving the store, I wasn't quite sure how I felt. I think my friend might have been somewhat interested, but I didn't feel bad because I moved faster than he did. I saw an opportunity and took advantage of it. She didn't show any hesitation, so I assumed I had a green light. I didn't think to ask her for her number. I hope I hadn't made a mistake by not doing so. I didn't ask because I was really trying to find out if she had a man. I assumed if she did, then she either would not have taken my number or it wasn't that serious. I guess what I didn't consider is that she would take my number and not call. Nevertheless, I was leaving the decision in her hands to call. Only time would tell if she would.

FIRST DATE

OVER THE COURSE of Christmas Day I anxiously awaited her phone call. Like me, I assumed she didn't have anything to do and would call. The call never came so I spent Christmas day going through the motions. I was from house to house visiting family and friends. I popped in to see my daughter for a few minutes but didn't spend a lot of time there. I ended the day where I typically would, at my play dad's house, on the couch watching football and drinking. I was anxiously waiting on the phone call that never came. In the back of my mind, I figured this wasn't going to happen. Women like her didn't get with guys like me. I don't know why I allowed myself to be so critical in that moment. I had already come to the conclusion that she wasn't going to call and it was only wishful thinking. I heard the familiar voice speak. It was the voice that would have me doubt that anything positive could occur in my life. The voice killed any encouraging signs every time, so I started to believe the awaited phone call would never happen. I didn't want to give hope a chance.

She finally decided to call the next day. She said she thought it would be inconsiderate to call on Christmas day because she assumed I would be spending time with friends and family. She didn't want to interrupt that time because she had only just met me. If only she had known I was stalking the phone the day before waiting on her call, she probably would have called sooner. There's no way to truly explain the excitement I felt. Why was this call so important to me? I didn't have a problem meeting women. I was only single because I hadn't found a woman that would accept me the way I was. The alcohol was an issue that most women were not willing to sign up for. Did I think she would be any different? Would she accept me like this or demand the change I needed. I was unsure how we would work through all that, but the call was the start. It was important because it gave me a reason to be hopeful. Deep within, this hope was bubbling to the surface.

When she called we got all the formalities out of the way. She was still in school at Jackson State. She looked young but I didn't realize she was only nineteen about five years younger than me. I started with telling her about my family starting with my twin. We found out there were definitely some commonalities between us. We both were twins. She was identical and rather close to her sister even though Kenny and I looked nothing alike. There were four of them, all girls, whereas there were four of us, all boys, and both our moms' names were Mary. I also went ahead and told her I had three kids so that she could decide if she wanted to deal with a man with children. I left the choice to her. I didn't want to start out with lies. She asked me did I drink and smoke and I said yes, occasionally. This conversation carried on for about an hour and then we made plans to meet later that same night at her place.

I went to her place which was on the nicer side of town. I knew I would have to be careful because I didn't want to get caught drinking and driving. The cops on that side would have none of that. As I pulled in, I got rid of my beer, leaving it on the ground outside of the car. I was nervous not really sure what she would think of me. I thought I pulled myself together rather nicely dressed in a nice pair of corduroy slacks, a sweater, boots, and a nice hat. I hoped she noticed that I put in some effort to make a good first impression. As I approached the door, I put out my cigarette and popped in a mint. I strongly considered turning around because I didn't think I deserved to be there, but I knew the plans must go on.

When the door opened, I immediately thought it was her, but was introduced to her twin sister. Wow, they looked just alike, at least initially. Then she appeared. She was much more relaxed than when I saw her the first time. She didn't seem so stressed. She was wearing a short dress, couldn't have been longer than a long t-shirt. She was still as beautiful as I remembered and just as sexy in that dress. After her sister went into the other room to give us some privacy, we hung out on the couch and talked most of the evening. Now I could sit back and observe more than just her physical appearance and get to know the woman behind the face. She was very intimidating but what I immediately liked was that she was both a sharer and a great listener so I felt really comfortable talking to her. I could tell she was very intelligent just in the way she talked and put her thoughts together. She wasn't a woman of many words but she was very thoughtful about what she said. Tina was sheltered and wasn't exposed to the streets. She didn't drink, smoke, or hang-out although she was young and living on her own. She was pretty settled and level-headed. I really liked that about her and thought that she would be good for me. I just didn't know if I was good for her. After staying over for a few hours I decided to go home. We made plans to see each other soon and I left.

The next time we met I decided to show her off. I guess she was becoming my little trophy and I wanted her to meet a few people that were special to me. God I was moving fast. I'd never done this before, but no one had made me feel like this before.

It was the holidays so we went to see my mom, my friend's mom, and my play dad. Everyone thought she was really nice. I'm sure they were wondering the same thing I was, what was she doing with me? She was so comfortable in any setting I took her to and got along with everyone. They all seemed to love her right off the bat.

SETTLING IN

I TRULY BELIEVE Tina was sent by God to help bring me out of the lonely place I had fallen into. She was definitely different. On our first dates, I took Tina to a number of places that I thought she would be okay with. We went to the pool hall, hung out over some friends' houses, and rode around. She wasn't impressed. She quickly noticed I drank a lot because of the number of stops I would make to buy beer. I knew she was different because what I was used to doing was not acceptable to her. That's when I learned you can't change what you tolerate. I thought about what Momma Crump said to me about the women I dated. She said, "Keith, you don't need a woman that's going to accept what you do and say nothing about it. You need a woman that won't accept it and challenge you at the same time." And that's exactly what I had. But she did it in her own way. It was subtle. She was never in my face about the drinking though she would discourage any behavior resulting from it.

As my relationship with Tina began to grow and we became more serious about the direction we were headed in, I struggled with something that I couldn't open up about. I struggled with love. I was stripped of it because the addiction made it impossible for women to love a man like me. This had always been the case. Love hurt and I couldn't give something I didn't have. I was not saying I couldn't love a woman like her or I didn't want to experience love with her, I was just afraid to fall in love because I knew how the story went. It always ended with drinking getting in the way, making it hard for any woman to love me and stay in a relationship with me long-term.

I was even asked by one young lady before she ended our relationship how could I honestly love her and not love myself? She was right, I couldn't love myself, not in the state I was in. Drinking was the only thing I did love and it was the one thing that kept me from moving forward in any of my previous relationships. The life I was living made it hard to fall in love but I tried to show love as best I could.

I tried to do everything I could not to fall deeper for Tina but she made it impossible. The kind of attention and affection I was getting from her was making it difficult to resist her. When you are experiencing something you have never experienced before, it makes it impossible to not want it. The more time I spent with her, I realized I didn't to want to be away from her. I remember the first time she celebrated my birthday. She pulled out all the stops to make sure it was extra special. Before then birthdays were no big deal for me, just another day of the week. On the night of, she prepared an extra special dinner, going to great lengths to set the table with candles and nice dinnerware. The gift she purchased was even more special, a nice pair of Masonic earrings. It was very thoughtful and extremely unexpected. I remember going to work the next day bragging about it. The guys gave me the blues saying I was definitely in love. Maybe I was, but I just didn't know how to express it.

Everything about this woman was absolutely amazing! The way she would talk to me and the way she would listen to me was unlike anything I'd ever experienced. The way she corrected me was never harsh or brutal yet she was not afraid to challenge me. I was being taught how to handle my situations differently, by someone I hadn't known long. She had an unbelievable impact on me. She wasn't afraid to enter my world and find out who I was and why I did things the way I did them. She was willing to help me make the right improvements.

I felt at times I had to protect myself because if the relationship didn't work out, then what? I was experiencing a different type of woman on a totally different level. I'd previously been in relationships with women who treated me like they were better than me. They acted as if they were doing me a favor by being in a relationship with me and the way they treated me oftentimes showed up in the way they spoke to me. But Tina spoke from a totally different place. Her words didn't hurt, they helped, and were genuine, comforting, encouraging, and nurturing. She said things at the right time, with the right intentions, and that made the difference. This relationship was so good for me I was scared that it wouldn't last. I remember asking, "Tina, am I just something to do until the right man comes along? Are you here because you feel sorry for me? You are sacrificing this very moment and possibly your future by being with a man like me. I don't understand, Tina. You are headed in the right direction. I'm just a man with a problem and at this point, I only exist. We don't fit each other's lifestyles. You don't fit in my life and I'm trying to see how and where I can possibly fit in your life."

I'd stopped caring about what people thought about me a long time ago. I thought about my situation like this; people travel to prisons to visit someone who is in jail only to tell them through a glass window that they are nothing! People saw me every day in my prison, dealing with my issues, and struggling with alcohol. They saw that I needed help but still treated me as if I was the worst criminal in the world and I deserved to be where I was because I was an alcoholic. They treated me like the punishment fit the crime which is why I stopped caring about people and their feelings toward me. People showed me how they felt about me through their actions towards me.

I could go on for days talking about my life and the things I was facing. The thing I loved about Tina was that she listened to everything I said. The night we had this conversation she finished it off by saying, "Keith, I'm not the type of woman that will tear you down. I will only build you up. I'm interested in getting to know more about Keith Jenkins. You haven't mistreated me; you are a gentleman, you are a man of good quality and character, and I can't say that about most men. I'm willing to help you but you have to want to help yourself. When you aren't drunk, you are a man I can see myself being with.

This is the man I want to get to know more about. I can't do the person you are when you are drunk. You become someone that I don't know."

The more time we spent together, the more I felt I needed her. Just being around her gave me the hope I needed. I remember asking Tina what she looked for in a man and what qualities she required. She said she didn't want a man that drank, smoked, or had kids. I think the blank stare on my face pretty much said it all. I had all of the above, so I asked, "What makes me so different that you are willing to give me a chance when all these things were on your list?" Her words were settling, "Keith, you are a good man with a problem; that's not unheard of. You have great qualities and I see a lot of potential. If you are willing to try, then I'm willing to help and not let your problems get in the way of what could be."

"But I don't see what you see." That was the only way I could reply to what she'd said to me.

I vividly remember her saying, "It's not always for you to see."

I was just the opposite in regards to what she was looking for in a man, and that showed we were at different stages in life. See, I was looking for a pretty face, sex, and a relationship that was not too serious. I didn't have much of a list when it came to standards other than being a lady. My previous committed relationships proved quality and standards didn't matter. I can always look back at these relationships as a reminder of how life was for me. We just weren't compatible but I was lonely and looking for a woman to fill a void; I accepted anything.

I know she heard me because of the way she replied. "Keith, you have qualities–everyone does. But since you weren't willing to change, you accepted anything, but it didn't work when it was you who needed to change."

It's as the saying went, some relationships are there for a reason, a season, or a lifetime. I had definitely experienced some reason and seasonal relationships. They had a purpose, which had been fulfilled, and had been dissolved. Was this a lifetime relationship?

There's nothing in this world like having someone believe in you during a time when you don't believe in yourself. Tina and I had a great relationship under the circumstances. Considering the fact I had a problem, we were able to still establish a functional relationship and have fun with it. Tina became more than just my girlfriend; she became my best friend and a life coach. At some point she even started calling me 'Sweetie'. I was thankful to be her sweetie because she sure was my sweet thing. That was my new name until I was in trouble, then I was Keith. And If I was ever Keith Jenkins, it was serious. All in all, Tina had the ability to reach me and not just physically, but mentally as well. That helped me to understand the importance of being in control of my situation and not letting the situation control me.

When we started saying "I love you," I believed she fell in love with my potential because there was nothing else about me for her to fall in love with. I wasn't a bad man; I was just a man with a bad problem that was out of control. I had an addiction and it was taking my future opportunities from me. It takes a special kind of person to look past all the bad and see the good in someone; to love someone who had nothing to offer them. *How could someone so good fall in love with someone with such a bad problem who didn't even meet their expectations?*

Tina had the ability to look beyond the external. That doesn't mean that it didn't matter to her, it just means she placed attention on what she saw internally. She would always tell me I had great potential, good qualities, and I knew how to treat a woman. There were just some things I needed to work on but that didn't mean I shouldn't be able to experience love. Not everyone has the ability to look past the outward appearance, or past a situation to find the good in a person.

When Tina and I met it was a difficult time for her. She was dealing with the painful loss of her mother, and not long before that, her father had passed away. I've often wondered about us meeting during such a painful time in our lives after having experienced great loss. My father had recently passed as well and because our parent's deaths were close to each other, working through our losses brought us closer together allowing us to connect in another way. I remember the night we sat on the couch at her apartment talking about our parents and sharing how difficult it was dealing with their deaths. We cried together and the more I cried the closer she got to me, with my head eventually landing on her shoulder. I wasn't really able to cry when my dad died, I guess, because I was so angry, I had held it all in. But finally being able to release the anger and the pain, the tears were the start of the healing process. We dealt with death differently and it seemed like Tina laid all of her pain, grief, sorrow, and sadness aside to help me deal with my own.

I often wondered if her healing came through helping me. People grieve differently; some grieve in silence, some are more open expressing exactly how they feel because they don't want to be alone, and some have to seek help during these difficult times. I didn't seek it but it just kind of happened that way. While others may require a moment to themselves to get a handle on their grief, I turned to her for comfort. It's not often you find a person capable of helping another through their grief when they are dealing with it themselves.

Tina had a way of addressing issues with me that would make most people uncomfortable. That was true, tough love. She was able to have conversations with me about my children. It was a conversation that she approached very carefully so as not to upset me but to see what my intentions were regarding my children. I wasn't involved financially and I wasn't spending any time with them. She wanted to know when I was going to step it up and start taking care of my kids. I had the same old response to this question, "I do for my kids."

She was very adamant in answering me, "Keith, do more!"

I think once she saw I had no type of involvement with my kids' mothers, it made it easier for her to have the conversation. Initially she asked a lot of questions because she had to make sure I was telling the truth about my involvement with them. I'm sure there may have been some doubts early on. I was a man with children by three different women. I'm sure she thought something was going on with at least one of them. She told me I needed to develop a meaningful relationship with my kids. This was possible to do without having to be so involved with their mothers. I was thinking *how is that possible?* I had done a pretty good job of pushing them out of my life, how could I possibly build any sort of a relationship with my children and their mothers now?

Tina didn't have to be as outspoken about the situation with my children as she was; she had no personal ties to them. What she was trying to get me to see was that my actions and the picture I was painting for her didn't look good. She explained to me that if we were to ever have children, I was already sending the wrong message. I will never forget what she said because it made so much sense. To have Tina express her concerns to me that I was doing something that could possibly affect her in the future showed me that not only did she care about my decisions impacting my kid's lives, but also what impact it would have on her if this relationship was to progress. She held me accountable and let me know she was not going to sit around and allow the same thing to happen to her.

"Keith, I don't know the kind of women you are used to dealing with, but what you are doing isn't acceptable at all. Your children need you! Keith, how can you be a good man to me and be a poor father to your children?"

She was not going to stand by and let me show her I could be a good man to her and abandon my kids even more. This put Tina miles apart from any woman I'd ever dated. What she said hit deep and hard and I don't think there was anything I could have said to convince her that I could be a good man to her and not be involved with my kids. I wasn't expecting to hear what she said, but I had to accept it. She wanted me to get involved in their lives.

What she said definitely caught my attention, which caused me to think about what I'd done. In my mind I felt that I had made the right decision based on my condition, but clearly I had handled the situation wrong. Tina was adamant and believed if she accepted this behavior from me, then she would accept anything. The way I was operating back then, especially with my job was unacceptable. I was making enough money to take care of me and my responsibilities. My check was just enough to maintain me and my habit. As our relationship progressed, Tina began to notice a pattern of how the morning after a night of drinking went for me. Whether or not I went to work would be determined by how much I had to drink the night before. This was most obvious on those Mondays following a pay Friday, the weekends when I would go on drinking binges that almost impaired me from going to work at all. This became more frequent and something I could not control.

When Tina noticed that drinking during the week was affecting my ability to work, she began suggesting that I cut back or stop drinking until the weekends. Of course I told her I had it under control and didn't have to drink during the week. That's what she wanted to see change. Our relationship was a little testy at times, but somehow she managed to hang with me. We didn't have that on-again, off-again type of relationship. We continued to work on it even though the drinking continued to cause problems.

I know this may sound crazy but if drinking was a woman, I could see how she would have felt threatened by my new relationship with Tina. She would have been fighting hard to show me that she was the woman for me and that she wasn't going anywhere. To be honest, I wasn't feeling her anymore; I just couldn't leave her alone. Tina was fresh and new, and she had become the perfect distraction, helping me to take my mind off of my troubled relationship.

Now if Tina had known this other woman existed, I would not have made it this far because of her values. She was not the kind of woman who would be involved with a man knowing he was in a relationship with someone else. She certainly she would not have been willing to accept that kind of behavior and stay in a relationship that was not healthy. I was now done with being a two woman man. My relationship with drinking was unhealthy and I no longer had a desire to be in it. I only wanted Tina. I wanted what was good and made me feel good and Tina did exactly that, but I couldn't have it because of the drinking. My addiction was something I didn't want anymore; it wasn't helping me, and it wasn't good for me. I just didn't know how to get out of it.

THE PROPOSAL

*D*O YOU JUST *wake up one day and say, I'm going to propose. No, of course not.* My love for Tina had been growing intensely over the past few months and I knew she was someone that I could spend the rest of my life with. I believe it was the first time she cooked dinner for me that I knew this woman was going to be my wife, but I really didn't think I would be popping the question so soon. I knew if I wanted more with Tina, then I could have it, but only if I ended my relationship with drinking. This was my desire, but I wasn't sure if I was mentally able to do so at this time. Even though the relationship with drinking was not good for me, I just couldn't break it off. My drinking hadn't slowed any and I'm sure she hadn't seen any of the improvements she was looking for, but for some reason, even though I wasn't where I needed to be, I felt like I had to ask her to marry me.

Some may have thought it was too soon to get engaged seven months after we met, but I knew this woman was my wife. I wasn't disputing anyone's opinion of our getting engaged because as a man I knew the kind of woman I wanted. I found her and she was exactly what I needed. To me there was nothing to dispute. Either I was going to live in misery because I missed my opportunity for happiness listening to someone else's opinion or seize the moment and be happy because I listened to my heart.

I used to sit around listening to older men and the wisdom that I got from them concerning marriage. This helped me with my decision in regards to the timing of when I should have proposed. In our conversations, they said young men blow it because of how they view marriage. We can have a good woman and lose her because we think we have to have it all together before we pop the question. They weren't saying it's like church, and you could just come as you are, and a woman would accept anything, so don't do that expecting to get a 'Yes'. You might actually get turned down. There is some level of expectation that a woman has when you ask her to marry you, but each scenario is different. There is no blueprint on what is or isn't acceptable. They pointed out that some things are not designed to be put in place alone; some things are designed for the couple to put in place together. However, you have to be careful because the things that you know need to be put in place may cause you to lose focus on what's already in place. So while you're trying to fix issues you may be having you don't want to lose focus on the relationship itself.

On the day of, early that morning I talked to my mom about my feelings for Tina and what I was planning to do because I wanted her approval. Mom had always told me that she was very grateful for Tina because she saw the positive impact Tina had on my life. Mom said she didn't worry as much when I was with Tina because she knew there were things that Tina just wouldn't allow. She was very excited for me but her biggest concern was my drinking. Mom knew firsthand the effects alcohol could have on a marriage and how devastating it could be for the spouse living with an alcoholic. To this day my mother had never said a negative word about my dad and his battle with drinking however she wanted me to know that drinking could ruin a relationship.

My mom said to me, "Keith, Tina is a good woman and she is good for you. If you're not going to do right, then don't waste her time!"

My mother was my biggest cheerleader. Even though she was very concerned about my drinking, she still believed that I would make a great husband when I put the bottle down. She said I couldn't have both worlds because the two worlds don't belong together. I took heed to what she said, and even though I hadn't made up my mind to quit this day, I was going ahead with the proposal. Tina and I could work through the other issues together.

I had the whole day to think about how I was going to propose to Tina and honestly, I had no idea what to do on my budget. I couldn't do much but I wanted this moment to be perfect. Hearing my mother when she said, "Son, be yourself", was the best advice, because I didn't have to try to be someone I wasn't. I would do what I could with what I had which took a lot of stress and worry from me.

After talking to Mom, I sat around most of the evening waiting on Tina to get off work. I was preparing the house and more importantly myself mentally for the biggest question I would ask in my life. I was so nervous anticipating her answer. There were so many negative thoughts going through my mind. What if she rejected my proposal? I knew my drinking would be a major concern for her and the determining factor.

When Tina came home from work that night, I was as romantic as I knew how to be.

As she walked in the house from work, I began to ask her how her day was. I guided her to the bedroom and told her to relax on the bed because I had something planned. She had a peculiar look on her face because she knew I was up to something. I don't think she suspected what was getting ready to happen.

As she was getting settled on the bed unwinding from her day at work, I began to light candles that I had previously set out, and draw a bubble bath for her. After dimming the lights and guiding her to the bathroom, I nervously proceeded to undress her when she asked, "Ok Keith, what's going on?"

I ignored her, while continuing to undress her, then I gently placed her in the tub. There were just enough bubbles in the water to fall over the edge. Once she had a smile on her face and after making sure she was comfortable, I took a seat on the floor beside her. I don't think she could have imagined what would come next.

At the start of my conversation, I asked her to just listen because I had a lot to say. Earlier that day I had rehearsed in my mind what I would say, but I quickly deviated from that script once the time had come. I began by trying to explain what I was feeling. I got really emotional sitting there on the floor telling her how much I loved her and how my life had changed since we'd been together.

I said, "Tina, knowing you has made me want to do better because better is what I want you to have. Tina, I'd like to think that somehow you believe in me…"

Before I could get the next word out, she interrupted and said, "I do but I still expect to see a lot more improvements."

After this statement I was scared of what her response was going to be. It was a possibility she would reject me which would have been devastating. This conversation went on for quite some time before I built up enough nerves to pop the big question.

"Tina, I know you've taken a chance on dating me when I know you could've had much better. I'm asking you to please take a bigger chance and give me the chance to be your husband." I was on the outside of the tub on both knees when I asked, "Tina, will you marry me?"

When I pulled out the ring to present it to her, she sat up in the tub like, "Is this for real?" Amazed and looking me straight in the eyes, what I heard next were the sweetest words. She said, "Yes, Keith, I will marry you!" Really! I was hoping for the best but prepared for the worst but it was an absolute joy to hear her say, *Yes, I will marry you!*"

Tina's acceptance came with some conditions and a lot of concerns. We had a long heart to heart that night about us, but overall I was a very happy man. She said "Yes" and that's all I had been waiting to hear.

THE ULTIMATUM

ALTHOUGH TINA HAD accepted my proposal I knew it came with conditions. She was not going to just ignore my drinking problem and marry me in my current state. She had made that very clear. I had to get my act together. I don't know why it was so difficult, but it was. *Did I think she would just ignore the bad behavior and the continued abuse? Was I really the type of husband she wanted? Is this really the life she dreamed of for herself?*

I know there were embarrassing moments for Tina being in a stressful relationship with an alcoholic. My aggressive behavior and lack of concern were some of the things I was dealing with at the time. I wasn't getting any better, which again made me question how long Tina would stick around waiting for me to change. I noticed it didn't take long for her frustrations to surface because her reactions towards me had changed rapidly. Had her tolerance changed of the things she would and would not accept from me? This could have been her way of warning me she was at her wits end and was no longer going to deal with this anymore.

The Sunday I dropped Tina off at work was the day I believed she'd had all she could take with my drinking and my behavior. When I dropped her off at work she said, "Keith, please be on time picking me up. I have a paper due and I need to go to the law library to finish it up. I really don't need you to be late!"

I went to my mom's house to spend the day there; I had no intention of getting drunk, but I guess I never did. I had only planned to have a few drinks and play a few rounds of dominoes under the tree with some of the fellows; but not get drunk. Consciously, I don't think I was aware of what a drinking limit was. I never monitored how many beers it would take to send me over the edge or how much was too much. It wasn't something I paid attention to. Even when there were important things that required my attention, I never gave drinking a consideration. I would never say, oh let me tone it down because I have this to do or that to do. I would drink at will and eventually lose track of time not concerned about anything else that was relevant or important.

I was late! By the time I arrived to pick Tina up the store had closed. I was late but not enough to get in trouble, or so I thought. The moment she saw me, she knew, and was clearly upset. I had been drinking and not just drinking, I was drunk. *Why could I not follow a simple request without getting drunk? Had she asked too much of me?* Just be on time. The least I could do was arrive on time given I was in her car. All she wanted was to get off work and finish up her paper. Clearly, I couldn't follow one simple request without getting drunk. I was given the silent treatment until we got to the car which was when the arguing began. She basically told me, "I can't continue to do this. It has to stop!"

We went to the law library and surprisingly enough, the trip was uneventful. I tried to stay out of the way so she could finish as quickly as possible. I knew she was furious and at her boiling point.

I'm not sure why she let me drive, but she did even though I was in no condition to do so. I guess she trusted me even though she probably shouldn't have. I didn't have enough sense to take care of myself let alone take care of her. On our drive home, it was evident to her that I was in no condition to be behind the wheel, but we were close to home, so she continued to allow me to drive and swerve. When I almost ran into the concrete divider that is used to separate traffic, she knew something had to be done. Out of her silence, Tina began screaming, "Keith, what are you doing? You almost hit that wall!"

I could see the wall but my reaction was slow. My mind was in slow motion. I knew if I had hit the wall it would have hit on her side of the car. I yelled at her, "I see that damn wall. Don't holler at me!"

"Pull over!" she yelled.

I asked, "For what?"

She replied, "So I can drive; you're going to kill me."

I pulled over and she jumped out of the car, yelling and crying. I yelled and cursed, trying to defend myself even though my choice to drive under the influence had put us in great danger. I saw the hurt I caused and backed down so she could drive the rest of the way home. She cried most of the way, not saying anything until we got home. Then she said, "We need to talk."

Any man married or in a relationship dreads hearing these words from his woman because he doesn't know what's about to happen. These conversations can go anywhere, and be about anything, so I felt a bit of anxiety as Tina grabbed me by the hand and led me to the couch. We sat down and she began to cry more. It took her a minute to get herself together before she could say anything and then what she said blew my mind, "Keith, sweetie, I love you more than anything but I can't continue in this relationship if you're going to continue drinking. The drinking must stop now if this relationship is going to last! I will not marry you like this."

I can't say I wasn't expecting it or that I didn't see it coming. I was still hopeful this would have blown over in a few days and we'd be back to normal. Yet, I knew this time she was serious about ending our relationship if I didn't stop drinking. She told me it was difficult to be with me because my lifestyle was becoming unhealthier each day as I continued to drink more and more. She said it was taking a toll on her because what I was doing ultimately didn't fit in the direction she desired to go. She'd asked how could we have a future together if we're on two different paths?

On that day she gave me a life-changing ultimatum, "It's either me or the drinking, but you can't have both." I was between a rock and a hard place; I was addicted to the alcohol and in love with a woman I was on the verge of losing.

Tina and I had talked about this before but this time was different. I knew she meant it. I was in between wanting love and fighting an addiction which wasn't an easy position to be in. I was so torn that I began to cry because what should have been an easy decision was actually quite difficult. The decision I had to make would determine the future I'd have and the direction my life would go. She wasn't nasty with her demand; she came from a place of love. Looking into her tear-filled eyes, I saw the kind of woman that I've always desired but thought I would never have. I heard this woman tell me she wasn't going to leave me. I knew that she loved me enough to give me another chance to get it right. I knew ultimately, Tina would one day be my Mrs. Jenkins.

I don't know that Tina fully understood the addiction. I wasn't drinking out of habit. I was well past the social drinker, or someone who drinks after a bad day at work, or a stressful week. Initially drinking had helped me deal with my pain, but I was so far past that stage. She knew I had a problem and that I had tried to quit before but there would be no simple solve to fix this. Because we had been down this "I'm going to try to quit" path before and it hadn't worked, I assumed that she would want something that was more definitive, not just empty promises from me. She was no longer interested in me "showing" signs of trying to stop. We had already gone through that before.

Replying to the ultimatum had to be well thought out but I had no idea what to do. To contain my tears with her, I took a walk outside and cried out to God instead, asking him to help me stop drinking. Asking God for help felt selfish because the only reason I wanted him to help me stop drinking was so that I wouldn't lose Tina. I remember telling God, "I need help and I don't know what to do. Can you please help me?"

When I walked back inside the apartment, Tina was sitting on the couch, waiting to hear what I had decided to do. I remember saying, "I need help."

She replied by saying, "Okay, but this is it."

PART IV

REHABILITATION

The fact is many relationships should end. They are unhealthy, cause strife, and are just not meant to be. Sometimes it takes something better to come along to make you realize that the break-up was so worth it. You'll find that it not only restores health, and confidence, it will allow you to experience true happiness, so much so that you may become better than you were before. Sometimes you just have to go through the process to get there.

-Keith D. Jenkins

THREE STOPS

O N THE DAY I made a promise to Tina that I would get help to stop drinking I knew my world would change. Everything was riding on the outcome of this promise and I was going through with it no matter what. I knew it would be for my benefit and it was the only way she was going to stay in a relationship with me. She had given me an ultimatum and I had to comply.

I honestly thought looking for a treatment center was something I was going to have to do alone, yet I had no idea how to go about doing it. Neither of us had any resources other than a good old fashioned phonebook and our faith that would guide us in choosing the right place. Tina sat with me on the couch and together we thumbed through the phonebook until we found a number to a treatment center. I guess it really didn't matter who I went with so I made no considerations for the type of program, success rate, or cost. Just having Tina by my side made all the difference in the world. But she was not going to do this for me. Any phone calls that needed to be made, I was going to have to make them. Not only was she demanding a change, she showed me she was willing to help me as long as I showed her I was trying to help myself. We went over some general questions that I should ask before I made the call and then it was all on me. Some of the questions we wanted answered were—What is rehab like? How long should I expect treatment to last? What was required before I could enter? There were a few other important ones, but this was the gist of it.

I knew the initial phone call to a representative at the treatment center wouldn't be easy but I didn't anticipate the questions that would be asked of me. The very first one that I was asked was "Are you an alcoholic?" It made me sad and embarrassed because I was wrestling with reality. While I had admitted in my head a number of times that I was an alcoholic, saying it out loud made it real. Of course I answered yes, and then she asked, "Why do you think you're an alcoholic?" I wasn't quite sure of my answer so I simply stated, "Because I can't stop drinking."

Tina gave me her ultimatum on a Sunday. I called the rehabilitation center on a Monday, and Tuesday I was scheduled to check in. The process wasn't difficult; in fact, I think it was too easy and moved a little too fast for me. The nightmares and addiction I'd lived with for years would prayerfully be coming to an end today. This was a bittersweet day. It was bitter because my drinking days were over. It was sweet because I was excited about entering rehab. I was finally getting the help I needed. I had psyched myself into believing that quitting was possible. I felt that everything rested on this decision and if I didn't do it, death would be the end result.

I got an early start that morning because I had three stops to make before I had to pick Tina up from class so that she could take me to the treatment center. On my way to campus, I stopped by the cemetery to visit my grandmother. I wanted to let her know what was going on with me and what I was preparing to do. I told her I had a drinking problem that was out of control and I was finally getting some help. I remember telling Big Momma that I knew I was better than what I had become and for my actions and behavior, I apologized. I started crying and it felt like Big Momma physically wrapped her arms around me in an attempt to comfort me. It was so peaceful to stand there at her grave.

At her graveside, one thing came to my mind: I wanted to be FREE and I knew this was now a possibility. It was so comforting to be there with her. It felt like old times when I'd tell her what I was dealing with and she'd always peacefully sit and listen. Big Momma had the best advice and knew exactly what to say to make sure I was headed in the right direction. It was times like this that I really missed her. Thank God I could still feel her presence near. Just before I left, I asked Big Momma to pray for me because I was scared. I stood by her grave with my head bowed in prayer. As I stood silently crying, I could feel her powerful and effective prayers. I always knew she could get a prayer through. When she had finished, still crying, I thanked her for praying with me and for always believing in me. I loved my Big Momma and hoped I hadn't let her down.

I knew I could not check myself in without going by mom's house, so she was my next stop. She had been one of my biggest supporters. No one knows what it feels like to see a child go through hell and not be able to pull them out of it. Mom had seen it all and through it all she still loved me. I never wanted to hurt her any more than I did Tina or myself, she was just a casualty of my war. As we talked that morning, I remember asking her, "Do you think my ending will be like my dad's?"

My mother looked at me with a smile on her face before she started crying and said, "Your dad was a great man, even though he was an alcoholic. He was a good father to you boys but a husband with a bad problem. Your ending does not have to be the same as his. You can be anything you choose; that's all up to you!" By the time she finished talking, she was crying, I was crying, it was an emotional moment for both of us. I began to apologize for all the problems I had caused her, and I told her I would work extremely hard to become the man I once was. Then she said, "Keith, there is no doubt in my mind you can do this. You are a special child and you can do anything you put your mind to. You can do anything through Christ who will give you the strength. I love you, son." I still remember her words to this day.

My mom wanted to go with me but I knew I wouldn't be able to handle that emotionally so she didn't go. My mother gave me the greatest thing— wisdom. At that moment, her voice alone settled my spirit and gave me the assurance I needed that everything would be ok. She also gave me the desire to fight for what I believed in. Knowing that her prayers and blessings were with me was more than anything else she could offer.

My third stop was by the house of a gentleman that I referred to as "Pops". For all intents and purposes Pops had been like a dad to me after my father died. Unfortunately, he and I were able to relate to each other because he too, was an alcoholic. Despite that, he strongly encouraged me to look into rehab. He always said that I was different and had a future if I wanted it. Even when he was struggling with the horrible disease himself, he'd somehow find a way to speak a word to me and encourage me to better myself. What I loved most about our conversations is he always kept it real. I talked to him a lot about rehab and what I should expect because he had gone through treatment himself, but to no avail.

He'd say things like, "Baby boy, everybody's different. It's going to be tough, but you'll be fine." He told me what worked for him and the way he stopped. He didn't do it like other people. He said, "The problem most people make is that they try to stop all at once. Ultimately that's the goal, but first, you must condition your mind to gain control over the addiction. Once you have control, then you can start the process of stopping."

A lot of the things he said to me, I've cherished, because these things have proven to be life lessons. It's amazing how someone can find the strength to encourage you from within their own storm and not have a selfish spirit or seek anything in return. Although he didn't have to encourage me, he was able to speak those comforting words I needed primarily because he had been there-done that before. Not everyone has this ability so I was grateful that his words empowered me to push through.

My last stop was now to pick Tina up because the time had finally come.

DETOUR

Just like any relationship that has ended, you can remember the very last time.

T HE HARDEST THING for me to do was to pass by a store and not buy a beer, so I made a short detour on my way to campus. I was supposed to pick Tina up and afterwards head to the treatment center so I could check-in. But, on this particular day, when I was saying good-bye to alcohol, I had one last stop to make, because I needed that one last drink. I never really battled with whether I should or should not drink. If I wanted to drink, then I drank, and almost reminiscent of the first time, I stopped to buy a twenty-four ounce can of beer. I went to the bottom of the ice barrel and got it like I always did. Unlike previous times, I didn't feel bad because this was the last time. Tina was expecting me and I didn't want to be late, so I drank quickly. I remember thinking to myself, why and how could I give so much power to something so small? In my hand I held what had controlled most of my past and had the potential to control my future if I didn't stop. As I drank what was prayerfully my last beer, I couldn't help but wonder will I ever be able to overcome my desire to have this? Can I live without it? It was a harsh reality that only time would reveal its success.

This stop was different, so honestly I'm grateful I gave into temptation. Each stop along the way up until this detour had empowered me to feel bigger than the can of beer that I bought.

I didn't do anything to hide the smell or evidence from Tina that I had been drinking. When Tina got into the car, she gave me my kiss, smiled and very excitedly said, "Sweetie, I'm so proud of you!"

Her words along with everything I received that day were so encouraging and uplifting. We held hands all the way to the hospital and I remember turning on to Lakeland Drive when I said, "This feels like the last mile of the way for me."

She clutched my hand tighter and asked, "Are you nervous?"

"I am" I replied.

I felt overwhelmed and the closer we got, the worse I felt, but there was no turning back.

INTAKE

A S TINA AND I entered the facility, I was overcome with depression. I didn't realize I could move into such an emotional state so quickly. It felt heavier than any of my past experiences. *But why now? Why was I feeling so depressed?* I wasn't necessarily thinking about "the quitting" at this moment. All I could think about was being thirty days in this place separated from everything and everyone.

When Tina and I were sitting at the registration desk going through the intake process she could tell that I was feeling overwhelmed so she quickly took over. She became my voice, answering every question asked by the registrar. Clinching her hand, they continued to register me as if I were a child, unable to tend to myself. I felt so weak and powerless. The registrar was quiet, impressed with Tina and her efforts to ensure this process was as painless as possible for me. As Tina continued taking care of everything, I sat motionless. I did not have a desire to speak and wished this was all over.

It was official. The registrar had placed the admission bracelet on my arm and reality set in. I had reached rock bottom. I was a patient in a rehabilitation center being treated for alcohol dependency. Unlike me, everyone in this place seemed upbeat and extremely happy, *but for what? Who were they kidding?*

This was rehab and they couldn't be happy about being here? It seemed as though everyone was shuffling about trying to keep busy as if their problems did not exist. There were people trying to function without whatever they were addicted to. I felt like I was walking among zombies in a fight to reclaim their bodies. I didn't feel like I was better than anyone else here. I knew we were all the same; here to get help with our problems. We needed professional attention. For whatever reason we couldn't do it on our own and I was now going to have to come to terms with the fact that my problems required professional isolated help.

A key method used in treating people struggling with addiction was the use of prescription medications. Tina had adamantly voiced her fear of treating alcohol dependency with narcotics if it had the potential to create a new dependency later. She expressed to me, "If at all possible, try recovery without the medications. If you can't, then we'll have to look into the medications to see how addictive they are or if there are other options. I just really don't want you hooked on something else."

As Tina and I walked from the living quarters back to the front entrance, I had a meltdown. It was a moment that seemed to last an eternity and I couldn't forget. As we walked towards the exit and Tina prepared to leave, I didn't want to let go. I was overcome with my emotions and felt threatened by my new position. I asked her, "Are you going to leave me because I'm here?"

As long as I live, I will never forget her next words. *"SWEETIE, BEING IN HERE WON'T MAKE ME LEAVE YOU. IF ANYTHING THIS WILL MAKE ME STAY WITH YOU! DONT WORRY! I PROMISE, BABE, I'M NOT GOING ANYWHERE!"*

This was a very intimate moment for us although there were many onlookers around. As we were embracing each other, we had the attention of nurses, patients, and other people passing by because we seemed inseparable. I wanted her to stay in my arms forever. Thirty days felt like an eternity.

Tina was the light at the end of my tunnel and I was reassured by the flame that continued to glow in her. She had restored a little more hope in me because her love for me went far beyond the act of saying, "I love you." Her love was my strength; she became my voice. Her love was nurturing and uplifting. She understood me even when I didn't understand myself. She encouraged me to push beyond my potential and challenged me to achieve more than ordinary. To stop settling for anything, set achievable goals, and regain control of my life–that was my plan. Before she left she cried, which caused me to cry more.

I couldn't believe this was actually happening; my first day in an alcohol treatment center. My focus was no longer on my addiction or the length of time I was to be in the facility. It was on the incredible woman that I had fallen in love with.

Once I was settled into my room, I went out into the recreation area and that's when the nurse approached me and handed me a cup of small pills. She said, "Here is your medication. Take it. They will help you when you start detoxing which should occur within the next forty-eight hours." I immediately turned them down. She said, "Mr. Jenkins, you have to take the medication! The next couple of hours are going to be critical and you're going to experience hallucinations and the shakes. This will also help calm your nerves and possibly prevent seizures."

I apologized to the nurse and politely said, "Ma'am I can't take these because I'm afraid of the effects they may have now and later. I don't want to take them."

As we went back and forth, she said she would have to call the doctor because I couldn't refuse this treatment. I had to take the pills. Even though I was reluctant to take the pills, she was adamant and her patience with me had grown rather thin. I asked her, "Can I go to my room and take them?"

She yelled, "No! You will take them here so I can be sure that you took them!"

All I could hear in my head was Tina's voice saying try not to take the replacement drugs so I simply positioned them under my tongue to hide them. Afterwards, I opened my mouth wide enough for the nurse to see that they were gone. As I began to walk to my room, I was scared and confused. I didn't know what to do about the medicine. I wasn't sure if I should take them or not? In my room I wrestled with this critical decision, because I didn't want to take medication that could possibly affect my condition even more. God I wished Tina was here to help me decide.

I felt as if I were at a crossroads not knowing which way to go or what to do. I remember as a child visiting my dad in a rehabilitation center for this same problem. I can't forget the way he was acting; it was as if he was possessed by a demon. I remember feeling very scared for him. All of these things ran through my mind so I made the decision to flush the pills primarily because I didn't know how my body would react to them. It was then that I made a conscious decision that I was not going to rely on medications to stop drinking.

EMPTY ROOM

IN THOSE EARLY hours I sat in my empty room with my mind all over the place, thinking. My thoughts were so scattered. I thought about my life, why I was here, who was Tina with and what she was doing? But amongst all those thoughts that were playing in the back of my mind, God kept coming front and center.

It was in rehab that I began my relationship with God and the start of my prayer life. It's not that I didn't know who he was. I grew up in the church. I actually attended on a semi-regular basis but I didn't understand the difference in going to church and having a relationship with God until this point. I'd heard of folks going to jail and finding God, and I guess I was one of those folks. But it's in those darkest hours, when things become clear, when all the distractions of the world go away and you can hear him. I was invested in this place for the next thirty days and I had nowhere else to go and no one else to turn to.

It's amazing when I look back on this situation and how God showed me I could pray anywhere. I'll never forget what my Big Momma said when I made the comment, "I wish I knew how to pray." She said, "Pray exactly what's on your heart; God knows what you're saying."

In my room, there was no TV or distractions, and even the sounds outside couldn't be heard through the walls. I turned the lights off and it was so dark that I had to use the wall as a guide to get to the bed. I got down on both knees and began to pray. I still remember most of the prayer and how I began.

> *"Lord, my Grandmother said I can pray anywhere. She also said to pray exactly what's on my mind. Lord, I'm in a place where I don't want to be but there is no other way to get help. I've hit rock bottom; I've lost everything and the one person that motivates me the most, I may lose her too if I don't stop drinking. Lord, I don't know if You can or if You are willing to help someone like me, but I can't stop drinking and I don't want to drink anymore. Lord, this problem is too big for me to handle so I'm asking you to please help me."*

As I was praying, my mind seemed go back and forth from my prayer to things that I had experienced in my past, but why? Why now? Praying for me was one thing, but God showed me that this was the opportune time to seek forgiveness for past actions and behavior. It was not until then that I realized that asking for forgiveness was a part of praying for yourself as well. I began to ask God to forgive me for all the hurt I'd caused so many people. I asked Him to help me to be a good man, a good father to my kids, and a better son and brother. I'd let so many people down and I was seeking redemption. I prayed that this was my opportunity to come out fresh and new in this place.

After speaking those words I knew my prayer was life changing but I'm not sure if I believed that God actually heard me. It was a cry for help from the darkness that had surrounded me. After the prayer, I still felt depressed and down in my spirit. I thought about the journey ahead of me and the length of time I had to stay in the hospital. If the doctor treating me didn't think I was well enough to leave then I would have to stay longer.

One of the things I had to learn about prayer was that in order for it to work I had to have faith. At the time of this prayer, I had no faith because my situation was looking dire. It wasn't that I didn't have hope, things just were not where I would have liked them to be. I knew that God existed but I didn't have faith to believe that prayer worked. I knew I was feeling something other than Big Momma's wisdom leading me to pray. And although Big Momma had taught me the basics about prayer, I had to learn for myself that faith must accompany every prayer.

My desire to be healed, delivered, and set free was my reason to pray. But the things going on in and around me were making the faith part difficult. It was faith that led me to pray and I had to maintain that faith. I just needed to come to the realization that there was no problem or situation that couldn't be prayed about; I just had to have faith that God would answer my plea.

THE WALK

THE FACILITY I was in was not a resort-like treatment center for the rich and famous. It was not private pay. It was something that most insurance plans would cover, so posh was not what it was. But it was decent and one of the things I enjoyed about the facility was its amenities. The amenity I liked most on the property was the walking track. I found it to be my escape. I could be on it alone and no one would bother me. I went outside to clear my head not knowing the revelation that was yet to come.

The day was overcast. The skies were gloomy which was very indicative of the type of day I was having. As I walked in one direction, another patient was coming towards me in the opposite direction. I wasn't paying much attention to him but I noticed he was coming towards me at a very fast pace. I was trying to keep busy while I was waiting to see the doctor. I guess I was now one of the walking dead fighting to get my body back as well. As I saw him approach I could feel myself getting irritated. I wasn't trying to be rude to anybody; I just wanted to be left alone with my thoughts. The gentleman stopped walking and spoke, literally almost forcing me to speak back. I spoke in return and tried to keep moving along, but he asked, "Can I walk with you?"

"Sure, why not?" I responded, although I really wanted to be left alone.

To break the ice, he snickered and commented, "You a lil' clean to be walking, aren't you?" I guess I was but I didn't think about changing clothes when I checked in. I still had on slacks, a sweater, hat, and Stacy Adams. I laughed too because I hadn't paid attention to what I was wearing until he mentioned it. As we continued to walk, he began explaining how things worked, told me about the do's and don'ts, the good and the bad and what had helped him cope with being in there. Very carefully, he asked, "Why are you here?"

We were doing okay until he got personal. For some reason I began to cry and did my best to explain why I was there. This was an awkward moment for me because I was spilling my guts to a total stranger about my problems, saying, "I am an alcoholic and I am here to see if they can help me." Had I thought about it, I should have realized that he wasn't here on vacation either. I guess I was just focused on me and the pity party I was drowning in.

As we continued to walk, he asked, "How do you feel?"

I told him, "I feel like a big ass failure! I've lost everything. I guess this is what rock bottom feels like. I don't know if I can defeat this."

I wasn't expecting the reply I got. He said, "I know how you feel."

He let me know he could relate to my situation. He began explaining his story to me in detail. He said, "I'm a cocaine addict, not crack. It was something that started out innocent but later became a problem that got out of control. It started one night at a gathering with colleagues. I knew that cocaine was being used at the gathering but it wasn't something that alarmed me. It was being used in the back room of the co-worker's home. It was available just like beer and liquor were available to those who drank alcohol. One of my co-workers asked if I wanted to try a line. I didn't feel obligated because he asked, but tried it more or less out of curiosity to see what the hype was all about. When I tried it, I thought it would be something to mellow the night out but this became the start of a never ending nightmare."

"I can't be mad at anyone; I did this to myself. It wasn't forced on me. It was offered and just like they offered, I could have declined it, but I didn't.

For a long time I thought I was in control of it and thought I could use it and put it down when I wanted to, but that wasn't the case. I dealt with a lot of job-related stress and what I later found out about my addiction was the more stress I dealt with, the more cocaine I used until I became dependent on it."

I'll never forget how personal he got, explaining the effects his addiction had on his home life and how it ruined him personally, professionally, and financially. As he continued to explain, he told me how controlling the addiction got and how he began lying to cover it up. That's when he knew he had a serious problem. He told me that because of his addiction, he'd lost everything, a six-figure job, a three thousand square foot home, and his wife who eventually divorced him. He said he hadn't talked to his children in almost a year. Lord knows I wasn't trying to compare what he had lost to my losses, but to hear what his addiction had cost him was incomparable. The ironic thing is, everything that he lost, I was still trying to obtain. Talking to him allowed me to see that just when I thought my situation seemed bleak, there were others that were in far worse shape than me.

His story took me back to the prayer I'd prayed just before going to the track. I believe God was answering my prayer through this man. His testimony also served as a warning sign; it was a warning sign I recognized and had become familiar with. I ignored many of them up until that moment. I was absorbing everything that he said because this could have easily been me. Everything this gentleman told me I gave serious consideration because he seemed to be pouring out of himself and into me. His story both ministered to and motivated me. Did I want the type of success he had just mentioned? Eventually, yes, but I wanted my ending to be different. I wanted the happily ever after, but I felt sad for this brother because he had nothing but a story. I realized that if I continued to use alcohol, the destruction was sure to come. The only way I saw myself escaping this was to escape the grips of alcoholism. I quickly realized I would suffer even more loss if my life didn't change and at the rate I was going, death was a strong possibility. All of it weighed heavily on me because this could actually be me in a few years if I didn't take advantage of this opportunity and stop.

There were some other things that I realized as he spoke, one being that hard work would pay off. Why couldn't I have a wife with kids, a six-figure income, and a three thousand square foot home? He seemed like he was a successful man at some point. I can't imagine building all those things with the woman you loved to lose it all over something that you let control you. It sounded like some of the folks and places he went to only added to his problem as well so staying away from these would be a vital part of recovery.

His conversation was different; it didn't sound the same. I believe this gentleman was speaking from a place of anger and frustration. He didn't blame or attack anyone outside of himself though. He really seemed to be speaking from a place of concern. He sounded like a man who had made mistakes and was now dealing with the consequences of the mistakes. He seemed determined and ready to take on any and all obstacles that lay ahead.

As we continued to talk and walk, he inquired about the young lady that had dropped me off, asking "Was that your wife that dropped you off earlier?"

"No, sir, she's my fiancée."

"Man, from what I observed, you have it better than half of the people in here. To have that kind of love and support from someone special means a lot. It can make a difference and determine your outcome. No one wants to feel alone, especially going through recovery. Just knowing someone on the outside supports you and believes in you should mean a lot. Don't take that for granted." He continued, "I asked because I want you to see that you have one reason to stop–your fiancée! If I don't know anything about you, I know this young lady loves you. The way you guys embraced as she was preparing to leave caught the attention of a lot of people. And I'm sure it was not intentional, but it made a lot of people feel sad, because they're in here and lonely."

His next words were burned into my memory. "My brother, no one can do this for you! No one! You can have all the support in the world, but if you don't believe in your ability to stop, then nothing else will matter. This may be the fight of your life. If it is, fight like it is! Give it your all and make no excuses!"

This conversation really inspired me. He spoke with such enthusiasm and passion. I guess going into this I knew there was a mental aspect to recovery, but I thought it was more physical than mental. This gentleman told me that if I wasn't up for the mental battle, then I wasn't ready to fight at all. I needed to see someone other than myself in the same struggle and be strong enough to say, "I have been weakened, but my strength is in my character." This gentleman's quest to fight back against his addiction and his willingness to help someone in the process gave me hope. It also gave me a new perspective on how to fight.

I didn't get the gentleman's name but what was so amazing about our encounter was that he completely understood me yet knew nothing about me. I'm so glad that didn't prevent him from reaching out because left up to me, I never would have even spoken to him; I was so consumed with my own troubles. The final thing that he left me with was that you have to face your problems whether big or small, ignoring them is not an option. If you ignore them, you will find that they won't go away and could possibly consume you.

At the end of our walk, I felt a strong need to pray about what this guy had said. His words made me take a closer look at my situation. I went back to my room knowing in my heart that what had just happened had been for a reason. I couldn't stop thinking about the conversation. A lot of what he said made me sad, but I felt more determined about the journey ahead than I had prior to our conversation. I knew I had no reason to feel sorry for myself. I just wanted to tell God, *Thank You!* People can experience similar storms, but no two people's storms are exactly alike. Every storm has specific details and designs for that individual and at that moment, God allowed me to see that I had more to gain than I had to lose.

As I began to pray I remember thanking God. This guy had lost everything to his addiction. Considering, I didn't own a home; I was back and forth living with Tina and my mother. I didn't own a car; I was driving Tina's and my mother's cars. I had just quit my job to enter rehab and I didn't have a good relationship with my children or their mothers. I didn't have anything to personally call my own, so what did I actually lose? Nothing-And this is what I talked about to God. That actually made me feel good because now I saw that rehab wasn't a place of failure but the place that could be the start of my new beginning.

DOCTOR VISIT

I SAT IN the lounge area with other patients as I was waiting for the doctor. As I sat, I observed how this horrible disease affected others. I was the addict, so in any other situation, people were probably always observing me more than I was observing them. No one was asking me what I was in for, yet no one hesitated to tell me what their addiction was either. There were people from different walks of life, age groups, nationalities, and races. You name it and they were trying to recover from it. There was one girl as young as seventeen struggling with prescription drug abuse. This was actually her second time in treatment. The first time she had come via the Juvenile Court system as a part of her sentencing ordering her to be treated. This time her parents admitted her because not only was she using prescription drugs, she was drinking heavily as well. I thought this teenager was too young to be in a place like this but looking back on my addiction, seventeen was about the age I had my first experience. She should be enjoying the years of her youth and doing the fun things teenagers do, but instead, she was in this place. I guess it could have been worse; she could have been in jail or dead.

As I was sitting in the patients' lounge, I was able to observe how this place never stopped moving. People literally came out of one activity and went into the next. While sitting, I was also able to observe how the medication was affecting how patients were moving about. Some literally looked like zombies; they were really spaced out but trying their best to function. This reconfirmed my decision to not take the meds.

The nurse came to the lounge and asked me how was I feeling? She wanted to know if I wanted to join in on any of the activities like an aerobics class or sit in on arts and crafts while I waited to see the doctor. They had not scheduled activities and classes for me yet and she felt it would be beneficial if I did something other than sit around. She explained to me how the activities worked; classes were assigned to the patient according to their treatment and every treatment didn't need a particular class. I politely declined so I just sat there. I guess I looked odd sitting in the bleachers because I didn't want to get involved with any activity. Aerobics didn't appeal to me and making fences with popsicle sticks just brought back old memories.

The social worker walked me to a small conference room where she was preparing the chart for the doctor to see me. She asked me a series of questions which lasted about five to ten minutes and shortly after that the doctor came in.

As the doctor entered the room I stood up to shake his hand. After introducing himself, he said, "Please keep your seat." He asked how I was doing and if I needed anything. "Tell me a little about yourself," he said.

It wasn't funny but I giggled at his question. It probably wasn't the reaction or response he was expecting but I said, "I really don't know who I am anymore."

He said, "Well, I'm here to help you rediscover who that person is and in the process empower you to be better."

I remember him telling me it was going to require a lot of work and that this place was just a platform where the groundwork would began. He asked me what I wanted to achieve. The only thing I could think of was that I didn't want to drink anymore. I knew the kind of man I wanted to be; I just didn't think I had it in me to be that man. His reply was along the lines of, "You're off to a good start by seeking help."

He began asking me a series of questions to assess my mental stability. He asked if I was troubled with suicidal thoughts when I was under the influence or if I felt like hurting others. He asked if there was a history of alcoholism or substance abuse in my family. He wanted to know how much beer on average I consumed in a day's time. I averaged anywhere from a six to a twelve pack a day and more on weekends. I explained to him that beer was plentiful where I lived; just about everybody drank and it was rare to find somebody without beer. If one person had beer, we all had beer, and that's how I was able to drink that amount of beer because everybody around me shared in the same problem.

As the doctor analyzed the information I had given him, he said a lot of things that were quite interesting. He said most of my problems could be associated with my environment. He was not necessarily placing all the blame on the environment. But my problem would be harder to overcome because most of the people in my environment had the same issues. He said I needed to disconnect from my environment because it was not healthy and my access to alcohol was too easy. It would make quitting almost impossible. People who were in the fight to end an addiction needed to change their atmosphere. He said when your mind changed, your environment should also. It complicated the journey even more when you didn't disconnect completely from all access, because people associated with bad habits can serve as painful reminders of a troubled past.

Hearing what the doctor said was disturbing because in order for my recovery to be successful, I had to separate myself from my environment, my family, and friends. He felt they could be distractions. *What if I couldn't do what the doctor ordered? Did this mean my attempts would end in failure?*

As part of his evaluation, he began to talk about my mental condition because most of my problems started in my head. He told me that it was just as important to treat my mental health as it was my addiction. As a part of the program I had to go through therapy with a psychiatrist because he felt that treating the addiction alone wasn't getting to the core of the problem. For my therapy he wanted me to focus on finding out why I had such a strong addictive nature. Was it something from my childhood that was overlooked, or was this just something that aggressively progressed over the years?

As the doctor finished his evaluation, he pushed everything aside, turned to me, and looked directly in my eyes. He said, "There's not a person in here that can do this for you. This is something you must accomplish on your own, and our jobs are to help. You can get all the encouragement in the world, but if your mind isn't made up to make this journey a successful one, then the slightest thing can cause you to give up and quit. You've made the initial step by admitting yourself into the hospital. It's not going to be easy but I believe you can do it."

We finished our conversation, and what he said was something I needed to hear and stuck with me the remainder of the day. He wasn't coming from a negative place; he was speaking reality from a different perspective. I wasn't in a position to make my situation look like it was okay. I had a problem, and the reality was that, I had created this problem myself. What the doctor said to me was, "You can have all the support in the world, but support won't make the journey any easier. Support will encourage you and provide comfort but the journey belongs to the individual."

I know once I leave this isolated place and go back into society there would be some decisions I would have to make regarding my environment. I would need to stay away from any places that would cause me to relapse. I would also have to assess my crowd. Some of the people around me were there only as spectators; some rooted for me and unfortunately some rooted against me. The decisions I had to make would involve which people would remain. This had to be done because the doctor made it very clear that I had no future if my environment and the people within it didn't change. I had to make a drastic change if my life was to have the ending I desired. I began thinking about all of the good that would come out of quitting, and what type of position I'd be putting myself in if these changes could be made.

MY PRAYER

T HE RULES OF the facility were strict; as a patient I couldn't have contact with anyone outside of the facility for the first week. However, after returning from my doctor's visit, I needed someone to talk to. Tina and I talked on a regular basis. I also talked to my mom and Kenny every day. It would be a week before I could make contact with Tina or any of my family; this felt like forever.

I didn't know who I could talk to. I hadn't made any friends in the facility outside of the man on the track and I never even caught his name. I had no interest in talking to anyone else because they were all walking around like zombies anyway. I was isolated, stuck, and alone with a feeling of rejection. Returning to my room, prayer was the only thing I could do.

At that moment, I needed to know if I had God's help. The addiction made me feel like I was so far from God that He wouldn't be able to reach me. I knew that if I was going to be successful in this desire to quit my addiction, God had to help me. My prayer wasn't that repeated attempt to try and convince God to do something by saying, *"Lord, if You get me out of this, I'll never do it again."* No, this prayer was different because I had no control over my situation at all and my life was in jeopardy.

So, I invited the Lord into my situation. This was an awkward moment for me but I knew the timing was just right. I had never been in this type of situation before but I literally poured out my soul to God. I didn't have to search for the words to pray nor did I have to think long about anything that I prayed about. All I did was fall to my knees. I literally felt like I had someone next to me, kneeling beside me, and praying with me to help with every word that came out of my mouth.

Immediately I felt his presence and it was almost like Jesus was praying with me to God for me. I remember starting my prayer by saying,

> *"God, I'm sorry for what I have gotten myself into. Lord, I've been under the control of alcohol too long, and I want to stop. I've been tricked and manipulated into believing I can't live without drinking. Lord, I am convinced, I can't. I feel like I need it, but I'm to the point I don't want it anymore. I entered this place to show my family and the ones I love that I want help with my problem and that I'm very concerned about what's going on in my life. As of now, drinking has control over my life and I want my life back.*

> *"God, this problem is too big for me to handle. Lord, I remember my Big Momma said a long time ago I can ask You for anything if I believe with faith You will do it. Lord, I believe that in order for me to stop drinking, I need Your help. God, please take the taste of alcohol out of my mouth. Lord, I am afraid and if You don't help me, I won't make it. If you don't take the taste from me, I'll always want it. If You don't do it, Lord, I don't know how it's going to get done."*

I was not fully aware of what I had asked but I knew what I needed to see and before I ended my prayer, I asked God to show me that He was with me by helping me through this thirty day program.

TRANSITIONING

AFTER PRAYING, I felt that my encounters at the facility, in my empty room, with the gentleman on the walk, and with my doctor, had happened for a reason. I had sunk to my lowest point and knew this was not a place I wanted to be nor was this how I wanted to live my life. Mentally I was ready for a change. I didn't have to fight to believe in the change I wanted; the feeling came easy. So far, in my encounters, it was revealed to me why I had handled my problem the way I did and what I should do moving forward. I was not unlike most of the addicts that I had encountered today. Our journeys were similar but with different starts and stops. My stop was now.

It had taken this very humbling experience to get me here and it was here that I had learned the true meaning of humility. Experiencing this low point gave me a realistic understanding of what this meant. I learned that humility has its place in everything we do. James 4:10, says, "Humble yourselves before the Lord, and He will lift you up." Humility allowed me to enter this facility. I went in thinking that overcoming my addiction was something I had to do on my own. I thought this was something only I could do, but that's not possible. Without God's help, this would have been an impossible task. Humility placed me in the right position so that God could do the things I desired of Him. I only needed to acknowledge that I needed His help. I felt God had a design for my life but I would have to be elevated from my lowest point and experience all that I had to experience before he would put me in my proper place.

I went back to my room and prayed, and it was there that I told the Lord, "Thank You for this place." After what I'd experienced and what I'd been allowed to see, I hadn't lost a thing. I prayed for the gentleman from the track that walked and shared his testimony with me. I thanked God for this brother and his willingness to share. I asked that God would bless his marriage, his relationship with his children, and restore all that he had lost.

Rehabilitation was the place I began to transition. It was here where I really accepted my problem, confronted it, and was now doing something about it. God placed me there to get my attention and that He did. He used this place to separate me from the things that were familiar. There was a shift happening and I was being transformed into an entirely new identity. I was changing my mindset, my way of thinking and my attitude towards everything. God was preparing me to leave behind the person that I was, along with everything associated with the addiction. A cleansing had to happen. Nothing from my past could come out of here with me because I wasn't benefiting from it, and God knew I would not be in need of any of it anymore.

One of the first things that had to go was the spirit of negativity. It was fueling the depression and allowing no room for growth. Everything I looked at or thought about, I did so from a negative perspective. I didn't look at most things positively because I was harboring all this pessimism within. The reality was, although the situation might not be negative in and of itself, but my influence might have negatively impacted the outcome. I was most negative towards myself because I was in a bad place and thought this was where I was supposed to be. Once God began to cleanse me of those negative thoughts, I started seeing things differently. One of the things I saw first was that you could be in an unpleasant place and believe in a positive outcome. I no longer saw rehab as a bad place, and certainly not a permanent place, but a place of new beginnings. I no longer viewed it as the bottom but as the foundation for a new start.

There were people in my life who were constantly reminding me of how much of a failure I was. God revealed to me that I would one day hear those same people say, "I remember how you use to be." He gave me a glimpse of it to see it as past tense. It would soon be behind me as well and God wanted me to look forward to a new beginning. He wanted me to separate myself from the past and condition my mind not to focus on who I used to be, but to prepare myself for the man I was to be become. Everything the doctor said to me was the absolute truth. The thing about the truth was I wanted to dictate where it fit into my life. I didn't want to face it because I didn't want to deal with it but facing the truth was yet another part of my transformation.

After God revealed these things to me and settled my spirit, I was now ready to take on this thirty day challenge. I only had about twenty-nine and a half to go. After I had met with the doctor, had dinner or whatever they called that meal, and hide my pills for the night, I was ready for bed. I wasn't really sure how I was going to sleep this night, but I would make some attempt to try.

VISIONS

I WAS TIRED from the long day. Although I hadn't done any physical work, mentally, I was exhausted. There were a lot of things I had thought about over the course of the day. I had come to the realization that I was going to stop drinking and this was actually an accomplishable task. Now, I was ready to wind down. I had been in and out of the room all day but never really settled in. My luggage was still exactly where I left it when Tina and I had come to the room earlier. I don't really remember what we packed and I'm sure there were some essentials I needed, but probably nothing that had to be put away for the night. Since this could wait until tomorrow, I decided to go to bed.

After turning out the lights and navigating the wall to get to my bed in the pitch black room, I laid down and fell asleep. The dream started with me driving along a highway. I'm not exactly sure where, but there was a body of water over to the right of the vehicle. Oddly enough my vehicle was the only car on the road. There were three others in the car with me. They didn't exactly feel like people, more like the images from my past, but maybe it only felt like that because I couldn't really determine who the people were. There were two on the back seat and one on the front seat with me. I always assumed this was Tina since she sat next to me. As we drove along, we were talking and laughing and overall just enjoying the day. I was behind the wheel, going at a normal pace, not speeding at all. Typically when I drove I had a beer in my lap, and this day was no different. As we were driving along, out of nowhere, a sudden gust of wind air-lifted the car. It went flying nose-first, then flipped backwards, and finally landed on its hood, crushing all of us. We were killed upon impact. At the scene of the accident, an image approached me, reached out its hand, and said, "If you ever drink and drive again, this will happen!" *What had I done?* I woke up in sheer panic, sweating and crying. I was frightened by the dream, but the message was loud and clear. Was God speaking to me, and warning me? The warning was given to me in a way I couldn't ignore. If I ever drank and drove again, I would surely die.

I laid there for a minute in that dark room trying to process what it all meant. I was trying to rationalize if I was dreaming or if these were the side effects of the detox? It was a tiresome and restless night with a lot of tossing and turning. Because the room was so dark and quiet, I was finally able to drift off to sleep again.

It began with me on a journey. I was traveling to the surface of the earth. I was almost to the top, when all of a sudden I was trapped, beneath a cement sidewalk, crouched in a fetal position. It was dark and I could only see through a small crack that allowed a little light through. The space was so tight I could barely move. I saw people passing by but unfortunately they didn't notice me. I was scared and crying out, but there was nothing I could do to free myself. The only thing I could do was call out for help, hoping someone would hear me and save me.

My mother was the first face that appeared that I recognized. She had just walked across the crack that I was peeking through. It was in that moment that she recognized my voice as I was calling out. She looked around, trying to determine where my voice was coming from. When she realized she was standing over me she knelt down and began shouting frantically, "Keith! Keith! Son! Is that you?"

"Yes, ma'am, it's me. Please help me get out of here!"

She asked, "How did you get down there?"

It was difficult to hear my mother ask me that, but even harder to answer. I'm not sure if she realized what journey I had been on but now was not the time to explain. My mom tried everything she could to help me but it was pointless. Her hand wouldn't fit through the crack of the pavement. After several attempts, she went to get help and returned with my brothers. Each of them tried to pull me through, but their attempts were futile as well. It was not looking good for me because I couldn't be saved. It was as if the sidewalk was a retainer wall that kept me on one side of the concrete and my family on the other. They all began to cry because if I couldn't be saved, I would surely die like this.

After their failed attempts, Tina came rushing over. She lay down over the crack and looked through it with one eye open. Out of frustration, she yelled,

"Sweetie, can you hear me?" I heard her but chose not to answer. What was the point? I had given up hope. "Sweetie, can you hear me?" she repeated.

Through the crack I looked up at her; I was so close, but I couldn't touch her because the pavement that separated us was also the wall keeping us apart. All I could think about was how much I wanted her but couldn't have her. How close she was, but so far away. I knew that there was a future that had so many possibilities, just on the other side of this wall. If I didn't change my current situation, this future would never be. It would be buried with me underneath this pavement.

She kept crying out to me and I spoke and said to her, "Tina, you are the perfect woman! A man like me doesn't deserve a woman like you. Thank you for trying to help me out of a terrible place. Please don't waste any more of your time on me because you can do so much better. I'll only be a weight to bring you down. From the position I am in, I'm no good to you. I can't be the man you need and I'll never be the man you deserve."

Her tears were now falling through the crack of the pavement but I was still talking. I told her she gave me a reason to live and that because of her, my life had meaning and purpose.

"You've allowed me to experience what true love is. It's painful to say I'm sorry but from my position, sorry is all I have." Still looking up, I continued, "Tina, I wish I was in a position to wipe the tears from your eyes, but look at me. I can't even do that. Please go! I'm too far gone to be saved. Tina, I wasn't able to overcome the addiction; it was too much for me and that's why I'm in this position. Since I can't be saved, I will die in this position. Because of you and the love I have experienced from you, defeat doesn't hurt because I know I'm loved."

Tina, my mom, and my brothers continued trying to free me but their attempts were unsuccessful. I loved them dearly and thanked them for trying to help me out of the terrible position I was in. Tina kept telling me, "No, sweetie, you can do this! Don't accept this position as a permanent place."

In the dream, Tina said, "Keith, I promise I won't leave you! We can do this. But you've got to want it. I can't encourage you if you don't want to be encouraged and I know you do. Sweetie, I believe in you; that's why I'm here. Your family is here because they believe in you and support you too. They can't pull you through but they will support you!"

I said, "Tina, the crack is too small; I can't be reached!"

"Stop saying that!" she yelled.

"Sweetie, the crack isn't much, but it's a chance. You just have to have the will to pull yourself through. Most people don't have a chance, but you do, and it can lead to something better. Sweetie, anything is possible. Now please, reach, and grab my hand!"

As I looked up, I saw her hand coming through the crack towards me. "You can do it. Please, babe, grab my hand!"

With everything in me, I reached and the more I reached, the closer I got to her hand until finally we connected. Tina's tears were the water and I was the seed that had the potential to break through the crack of the pavement. I am amazed when I see a beautiful flower grow from a crack in the pavement. God can allow beautiful things to grow from unlikely places.

It was such a restless night. There was a lot of tossing and turning. I was trying to wiggle my way out of what appeared to be some type of restraint. The restraints were on tight; I wanted to be free but despite all my effort, I couldn't break loose. I couldn't tell how long this went on during the night, but I remembered being extremely tired from trying to free myself. Was I hallucinating like the nurse said I would? Should I have taken the medicine that she had given me when I was admitted? Was I in withdrawal stages? Was I losing my mind?

I felt strange getting up. It was a struggle to open my eyes; I was afraid to see what awaited me once my eyes were open. Slowly and cautiously, I opened them, hoping I wasn't caught in a bad dream. When my eyes opened, things appeared to be somewhat clear. I heard a still, small voice–a voice that I don't think I could have heard anywhere else, "I HAVE GIVEN YOU ALL YOU NEED TO MAKE IT. I HAVE YOUR ATTENTION NOW. DO NOT TURN AWAY FROM ME! CHECK OUT."

I was frightened by what I had just heard. I was also confused, because at this point, I was not sure from what source I'd heard the voice. Maybe it was my conscience dealing with me because of the long night I had just had, or maybe my mind was playing tricks on me? I was still in the clothes from the day before; my T-shirt was wet from sweating during the night. Everything I experienced in the dreams felt very real. I was exhausted from the dreams and they left me feeling like I had just been in the fight of my life. I didn't have the energy to get out of bed; every part of my body ached. I just wanted to lie there in a dark room and be left alone, but the longer I stayed in that bed the more pressure I felt to do what the voice commanded.

I wanted to move but I couldn't. I had the desire to move but I didn't have the strength. Something was holding me to the bed and didn't want to let me go. I was being taunted by the voice and pressure was building by the minute. I began to panic because the longer I stayed in that room the more it felt like the air was being sucked out of it. I was being forced to walk out and do something I was uncertain of. I knew once I walked out of the room there would be no turning back. I had to make sure of this decision because based on what I was feeling, I didn't think it was the right thing to do. Less than twenty-four hours in here and I was being told by an unknown source to "check out." I knew there was no way I could tell these people a voice told me to "check out." I learned during transitioning, I had to make a decision about which way I should go, and once I decided, I could never turn back. I knew I was displaying all of the signs and symptoms of withdrawal, so making the wrong move could get me reevaluated and more medications dumped on me.

Why did I now feel like I was better than this place and it was not where I needed to be? I was uncertain, but I couldn't ignore it anymore. I found myself standing at the nurses' station noticeably nervous and not fully confident I was doing the right thing. I knew I had to be careful in my approach. I stood in front of the nurse with my suitcase that I had never opened to unpack. I wasn't in rehab long enough to put away my things and settle in, but I stood in this woman's face to tell her I'd been there long enough and it was time for me to check out.

The nurse asked, "How can I help you?"

I didn't answer with confidence. "It's time for me to go."

She was cool about the situation. She didn't hit the panic button or get alarmed. She said, "No, you can't do that. You're going through withdrawals; it's the morning after, let me order your medication and after you take them, you'll feel better. It should help you calm down."

I wasn't trying to hear no for an answer. I said again, "It's time for me to go!"

"Mr. Jenkins, we're trained in handling withdrawals and that's what you are experiencing. Give me a few minutes to get your medication."

I tried to keep my composure but I was getting upset. The nurse and I went back and forth and I wasn't willing to give in. Finally, I said, "Who in the f**k are you, telling me what I can and can't do?"

That's when she picked up the phone and I overheard her saying, "His language has become abusive and he may need restraints!"

I could understand how the nurse must have felt when I said those things to her and how I must have scared her, but telling her "I'm ready to go" calmly didn't work. When the orderlies came to the nurses' station, I really didn't know what to think or expect, but I knew they had come for me. When they approached me, one of the orderlies asked, "How are you feeling, Mr. Jenkins?"

With my head resting in my hands and looking down, I said, "Ready to go; that's how I'm feeling!"

"Well, unfortunately, Mr. Jenkins, you're not going to be able to do that until you are well."

"I'm well now, and it's time for me to go."

When I saw the orderlies it took me back to a time in my childhood when my dad was in the hospital for this exact same problem. Was this déjà vu? Was the same thing getting ready to happen to me? I remember spending the night in the hospital with my dad and how he began saying things that didn't make sense. He seemed delusional and it scared me so I had no choice but to call the nurse. By the time the nurse arrived, my dad was ready to walk out of the hospital. She asked me to go stand in the hall and minutes later, three orderlies came to the room with what looked like ropes. I tried to go in behind them but the nurse told me to stay in the hallway until they could calm my dad down. It took about fifteen minutes for the orderlies to restrain him. When I was allowed to go back in, my dad was strapped to his bed. It was heartbreaking to see my dad like that; he was sweating and very upset because he had made up his mind, he was ready to go. When my mom made it back to the hospital, the nurse explained that my dad was hallucinating because he was going through withdrawals and that they had to restrain him for his protection. All of this ran through my mind as I sat and talked with the orderly, because I knew what his intentions were. By their measures, I was in no position to tell them it was time for me to go, nor could I say I felt God had told me to leave. They would definitely think I was hallucinating. I didn't think I would have had this kind of encounter with God, and I was not trying to use his name to get out of treatment. To be really honest if I had said God told me to leave I believe I would have been treated like my dad and restrained to my bed.

For whatever reason, the nurse called the social worker to come to the area where I was sitting to see if she could talk to me and calm me down. As long as I wasn't posing a threat to the staff or any other patient, the orderlies couldn't do anything to me so I had to keep calm. I wasn't angry, and I didn't want to harm anyone; I was simply ready to leave. The social worker tried to tell me something about the percentage of people who fail when they leave treatment too early. I wasn't trying to ignore her; I just didn't want to hear what she was saying. My mind was fixed on what I heard and was set on leaving. The social worker tried a different approach and began talking to me about all of the people who were depending on me to stay in treatment and get better. By no means was I trying to discount the value of what she was saying. I heard every word that she said about my family and how completing this program would be a better outcome for all of us if I stayed. I couldn't help but think about what she was saying; I wanted to get better, so I could be better, but for some reason I couldn't allow staying there to settle into my spirit.

I asked her, "Who's to say when I come out of here–after the thirty days have been completed–I'm not going to drink again?" I believe when I asked her this question she came to the conclusion that I was beyond convincing to stay. She wanted to know why was I so eager to leave and not give it at least a week. I was afraid to tell her or anybody about what had happened during the night for fear of being put in isolation because I sounded crazy. How could I explain the dreams and visions in a way that wouldn't make me sound crazy? I believed in what I had encountered during the night and I didn't think I had to prove the dreams to anyone because I didn't think the dreams were meant to share at that particular time.

The social worker asked me if it was okay for her to call the person I had listed as next of kin. I said, "Sure, why not? She has to come pick me up anyway." She wanted to call someone and see if they could possibly talk to me about staying because I was threatening to leave. I could hear her side of the conversation with Tina because I was sitting less than ten feet away. I was getting pissed and could feel my temperature rising. What she was saying was simply not right. I overheard her telling Tina that I was hysterical, and not cooperating with the nursing staff. She made it sound like I was a threat to the staff, other patients, and possibly a threat to myself. She told Tina that she had the orderlies on standby just in case I became uncontrollable. All I could think about was my dad when he was restrained to his bed and wondered if my behavior was anything like his. I tried my best to keep calm over what I heard her say about me on the phone because I was knew it would have Tina worried and then she would call my mother and have her worried.

She was over exaggerating and I wasn't behaving anywhere close to what she had just described. I may have shown signs of an aggravated patient but I was not who she had just made me out to be. Hell, that person needed to be locked up. Maybe she was simply on high alert because I was showing symptoms of an irate patient and that prompted her to say what she said. When I asked her who and what was stopping me from walking out of the facility, she reacted to my question sarcastically and said, "You will be arrested if you try to leave."

It was a criminal act if anyone tried to leave on his or her own recognizance? What she said didn't make sense though; I had checked myself in so why would it be a crime for me to check myself out? I asked her to explain how the process worked and how it would be illegal for someone to leave once they had been admitted to the facility that they checked themselves into.

She explained that most patients were admitted by court order, which meant their treatments were being monitored by the courts so they were required to complete the program. If those patients left or attempted to leave without authorization they would be arrested, and brought back to the facility, or taken to jail. Other patients were admitted by a family member who had power of attorney giving that family member the legal right to make sure the patient stayed and completed the treatment.

Why would I be arrested if I decided to terminate my treatment? I hadn't been ordered by the courts to be there. If I checked myself in, I should have the ability to check myself out. When she looked at my chart, she saw that I had checked myself in. She was now quite adamant about the downside if I was to leave the facility before completing treatment. Walking out could possibly be a death sentence, and the percentage of those leaving early usually resulted in failed attempts to self-rehabilitate or possibly death. The decision

I was faced with wasn't an easy one to make. If I decided to stay I would have ignored what had just taken place in my room and what I felt God was telling me. On the other hand, walking out could have possibly been an indication to Tina and to others that I wasn't serious about quitting and that I didn't want help. Either way, the decision was not going to be easy because I was not one hundred percent sure of the path I should take nor was I confident enough in my ability to choose correctly.

When Tina walked in, I remember trying to hold back my tears. At that moment, twenty-four hours felt like twenty-four years. It was a long time to be separated from the woman I knew I needed. I was not able to get to her immediately because the social workers wanted to let Tina know the importance of my staying in the hospital to complete the program. It was a proud moment because the one who had dropped me off was the one who had returned to pick me up. I believe Tina's thoughts at the time weren't to come and pick me up, but maybe she thought she was called to come to the hospital to help calm me down from possibly experiencing the withdrawal symptoms. When she came over to where I was sitting in the patient's lounge, she asked if I was okay. What Tina was really asking me was, "Are you sure of your decision to leave?"

I'm sure the social worker told Tina I felt like I was ready to go because I didn't take the medication and there was nothing helping me to cope with the withdrawal symptoms they thought I was experiencing. All I knew was I needed the woman who had just walked in. Apart from her, I felt defeated, lost, and without hope. For her to come back to the very place where she had dropped me off in my worst condition proved that I was a winner with this woman.

When she walked in, I realized this place had served its purpose and now I could leave it all behind. She asked me, "Are you sure, sweetie? Are you sure that this is what you want to do?" The only answer I had was "Yes".

So I checked into rehab on a Tuesday morning and after *one night*, on Wednesday morning, I checked out.

PART V

RECOVERY

Rehab is a process designed to treat and restore a person back to normal health, and whether the process is designed to be completed in twelve steps, thirty days, or one night will depend on you and God's plan for your life. After going through the process in rehab, it was now time that I recover. The difference in the two is one is the process and the other is within the person. After going through the process, it was I who had to recover.

-Keith D. Jenkins

AFTER REHAB

LEAVING REHAB, I remember being angry as hell at myself. This addiction had damn near stripped me of my identity and came close to labeling me as a drunk for life. I was vulnerable but optimistic. I was worn out and I needed rest. I looked bad, and because of the way my appearance had changed, I couldn't stand to look at myself in the mirror. I looked like I felt, horrible and defeated. I was actually looking like I was living. I was happy that I was home, but still afraid of the unknown. For so long, the spirit of addictions said to me through people and personal attempts, "You can't live without me; you need me. You're nothing without me."

That's what I believed until I heard the voice of the Lord say to me, "No fear comes from God." Those words ran through my mind for quite some time. I was still struggling through the process of not drinking and dealing with the fear that came along with it. When I began to pay attention to what was said, I realized that God was speaking to me. He was telling me that what I was experiencing in fear wasn't from Him. No one of faith can operate in fear. If God was telling me that He wasn't the giver of my fears, then who was? It was me allowing myself to focus more on failure and defeat than focusing on being successful. I didn't like getting drunk, but I loved to drink and unfortunately

I didn't know how to drink casually. Since there was no in between, I had to disconnect and get away from everything I was used to.

It had been almost twenty-four hours since my last drink, and for someone who drank every day, this was a huge step. The question now was how was I going to stop permanently? I knew it was going to be a long road to recovery but I felt like this time I could do it. The unknown was scary as hell because I didn't know what to look for or what to expect. My initial concern was that I had done this twenty-four hour thing before but ultimately started back drinking. I didn't want to have the same results again. I knew I couldn't start celebrating a twenty-four hour milestone just yet. There were going to be challenges ahead of me that were going to make the process difficult but it was now or never. I had questions that I needed answers to. Since I'd only spent *one night* in rehab, I'd forfeited professional help; so now I didn't have the medical community to help me through my journey. Tina, my mom, and my family were by my side, supporting and encouraging me but this wasn't their fight. This road to recovery was one that I would be traveling alone with them cheering me on along the sidelines. I was thankful to have the support, but the fight was mine.

When Tina picked me up from rehab, the first question she'd asked was, "Are you sure?" God knows I wanted to believe my answer.

With some hesitation, I replied, "Yes, I'm sure."

I felt really worried because I wasn't focusing on the moment. I was too worried about what was ahead of me because I was afraid it would end like my last attempt. As we got home, I asked Tina to go in and empty out the liquor cabinet. Great start, but mentally, I had to believe in the idea of overcoming alcoholism. Throwing away bottles wouldn't solve my problems if I just went back to the store to buy more.

That night as I drifted off to sleep, God showed me that he had put the provision of prayer in place for my recovery. It was in this dream that I saw my mother. She was in a garden surrounded by beautiful flowers rich with colors, tall magnificent trees, and lush green grassy areas. She was dressed in a white silk robe and she was kneeling to pray. It was a prayer so powerful that it sent chills through my body. It was in this moment that my mother appeared face to face with the Lord. She asked Him to extend his favor to her. She asked him with a boldness I had not witnessed before, "Lord, send me to hell so I can get my sons back!" The Lord tried to warn my mother of the seriousness of her request and the danger associated with it, yet he was amazed at her request and what she was willing to do for her children. I believe Jesus was waiting on my mom to ask Him to deliver her sons, but Mama kept saying, "I can't leave them there; I can't leave them there. They don't belong there. Lord, please give me the power and I'll go get them myself!" The Lord said to Mom, "Your persistence in prayer has shown great faith. Go! According to your faith be it unto you!"

I remember crying in this dream because I'd never seen my mother so determined that she was willing to go to hell and knock on the enemy's door to get what she desired. What this dream revealed to me was that some people believed my brothers and I were damned and under a generational curse because of my father's addiction we had no future. See we all struggled with something that could be pointed back to my dad's addiction according to others. And with all of the naysayers my brothers and I heard through the years, we allowed people to speak negative things into our spirits. These words didn't speak life, only death and damnation.

In the dream I saw my mother aggressively banging on an iron gate. It was a huge gate that was as tall as it was wide and looked like a never-ending wall. Her request was to speak to the devil. Crying and noticeably angry, she yelled a number of times, "Release my sons and their futures!" As my mother continued to bang on the gate, a loud click occurred that was so loud it had earth-moving effects. Slowly, the gate began to open and as it opened, I saw a lot of hands attached to arms reaching through a very small crack in the gate. They looked like they were waving in desperation. It was a wave for help and rescue. Then my mother, my brothers, and I were all back in the garden where I initially saw my mother praying. As I woke, I knew I had a mama at home that was on her knees praying for me and fighting on my behalf.

As the night wore on, my mind began playing tricks on me. I knew I was officially detoxing when I started hallucinating and having night sweats. I was too scared to sleep because I was afraid that my dreams would start back up again. I was in and out of sleep all night with Tina by my side asking me over and over again, "Are you okay? Are you okay? How are you feeling?" The night carried on forever. I felt like she thought this was a mistake and I should have stayed in rehab. Only time would tell.

I figured out very quickly that recovery is done one day at a time and is a continuous process. My desire to drink increased daily so I lived in fear of relapse. I had to make the choice to not drink every day while I was going through.

I stayed in the house for about two weeks not knowing if keeping myself isolated was helping or hurting me, but it was the only way I knew how to handle it. In a deep depression, I lost weight. I didn't have an appetite; there were days when I stayed in bed all day not eating and not even wanting to go to the bathroom. I cried a lot and understood that my future depended on every critical decision that I was making right now. I realized the position I was in was where most people gave up, that space between the prayer and the breakthrough; it was the place where the devil was busiest. I went through rehabilitation in the facility I was in, but I went through recovery in the apartment where Tina and I lived. I didn't have a guide because my recovery meant dealing with all that stuff on the inside. It was just me learning as I went along; I didn't know what to do or how to move forward in my attempt.

Coming out of rehab was easy, but the hard part started when the doors to rehab closed behind me. One thing was for sure; I could not ignore reality. Either I was going to turn back to my addiction or fight the temptation and stay away. Embrace victory or settle for defeat? Be a success or be a failure? This moment was critical for me knowing that my life could have gone in any of these directions. My desire was victory and success but I couldn't help but think about the losing side of what I desired. I knew I didn't want to dwell on the negative and be fearful of the unknown. If I let fear win, it would take me further and further from achieving my goals. It has a tendency to do this if you allow it to.

I heard me say, "I can do this," but actually doing it and living without drinking was something else. I noticed something about myself I hadn't noticed in a long time, I could be in control of my life and function without drinking. Victory and defeat and success and failure came from within the person. It was all up to the individual to choose what he wanted out of the situation he faced. Facing the unknown in any situation isn't easy.

Each day, trying to function without alcohol became increasingly challenging. Trying to hold a simple conversation was difficult to do. My mind would drift off and by mid-conversation you couldn't follow the point I was trying to make. I would be having a conversation about one thing and all of a sudden, my reply would be so far off subject that the person I'd be speaking to would ask, "Are you okay?" or "What does that have to do with what we're talking about?" It was embarrassing to say the least that I couldn't hold a conversation without being all over the place.

I didn't want to be a failure, but I was missing drinking so badly until it was all I could think about. There are a number of things that can contribute to a person's failure, including the individual, a lack of knowledge, not enough resources, the environment, and even the people the individual associates with. I didn't know exactly what success looked like but I knew it was something I wanted. I understood it wouldn't happen overnight; it doesn't just happen, it requires work.

As I worked through each day, I felt like I had been beaten beyond recognition, like a drunken mess, scared as hell, not knowing what to expect in my attempt to live without drinking. The people who were around me were some of my biggest distractions so I had to get away from them. I had to get away from all the things I was used to, and the things that weren't helping me as well. I couldn't do certain things because doing the same old familiar stuff had a memory attached to it, which could have caused a relapse. There were times though when I thought I could insert myself back into society doing old familiar things. Thankfully I had Tina there to help remind me of what the doctor had told me about changing my environment. The weekend following the week I checked out of rehab was the biggest game of the season and I thought I was strong enough to attend. I remember telling Tina, "Let's just go", "I can go and not drink, I know I can do this. We can just sit at the top of the stadium; no one will even know we're there". She was very adamant in her response, "No, you are not ready for that. I'll stay here at the house with you and we can watch the game from the couch if it's on TV. If not, you'll catch it next year. What's one missed game. It's not the end of the world Keith". I didn't like what she told me, but I knew she was right. I wasn't ready for that. Who knows if I would have relapsed had we gone? I had a made up mind to overcome the addiction even with all of the odds being against me, sometimes I just needed gentle reminders along the way to keep me on track.

I still believed success was achievable but it had to come from me; I couldn't depend on anyone else although I could see through others what it was to succeed or fail. My ultimate goal was to say I did it, but success did not come without a fair amount of challenges. In addition, it would require a lot of hard work and sacrifices, and potentially some loss. Sometimes loss was a sign of gain, and no one who is successful can honestly say they've never failed in their attempts at becoming successful. It could be disputed that I was going in the wrong direction, because I was doing it a different way. Some might say that the fact that I had checked out of rehab after *one night* was a recipe for disaster.

I had to create my own definition of success. To stop drinking was the ultimate goal and to live without a desire to drink again was how I would define it. To be successful in overcoming my addiction, I didn't want to be one of those people whom I've heard say, "I do it because I want to," or "I can stop anytime I get ready." Their definition of success may be–to get it under control–but for me to be successful I would have to live without the desire to ever want to drink again. Now getting there was my challenge.

Going to rehab was a step in the right direction and even though I only stayed *one night*, I still saw myself moving in the right direction. Some may say I failed because I did not complete the program. It was hard to believe that I gained in *one night* everything I needed from the program. In the weeks to come I would have to continue to remind myself that I got what I needed from rehab in order to be successful. I did not complete the program, but that didn't mean I failed. That's how I had to process it in an attempt to encourage and motivate myself so that I would have a successful recovery.

MOTIVATED

HOME IS WHERE the heart is, but for me it was where I would face my demons and sober up. Being isolated in my home was dangerous and scary as hell, but the need was greater than the risk. It was dangerous because I could have hurt myself or even worse, someone that I loved. It was scary because I was literally forcing myself to face a condition alone rather than being treated under the care of a professional. When I made the decision to go into that apartment and lock myself away, it was a hard decision but one I had to make. This was it. I didn't know what else to do. It was very important to stay focused, and the only way I saw it happening initially was to be in an isolated environment away from almost everyone and just about everything. I had to be in charge of what was going on around me. This was my way of creating an environment in which I could control who and what was coming in and out of my personal space. I had to separate myself from friends and work even harder to stay away from people who'd be working against me. I even had to separate myself from family. Yes, family too. It wasn't that I felt as if family was working against me or were not supporting me; I just didn't know how I would react in certain situations, so contact with others needed to be limited. I was moody, my tolerance level was low and anything would trigger me. I was not willing to take on this potential threat which could have pushed me to take a drink. That one drink could have been fatal.

As I was figuring out the keys to success on this road to recovery, I knew that encouragement would be very important to this process. The thing is encouragement can't be forced; it has to be received. It can't be taken; it can only be given. Initially, my perception of encouragement, I must admit, was wrong, because it was my belief that people *had* to encourage me especially those near me. It was good to receive encouragement from others, but I shouldn't depend on it. It was also unrealistic to expect to have my encouragement on tap, ready to turn on and off as needed, yet this was my expectation. I was seeking the motivation I needed from others because I was still struggling with figuring out how to motivate myself.

Don't get me wrong, there were many around me encouraging me along the way and I was encouraged from the support I received, but initially, this was overwhelming. It took a while to get used to, but as time went on, I became more receptive to the people and the encouragement I was receiving. It was hard at first and a very humbling experience. I was in a place where I felt I had no right to be on the receiving end of encouragement and certainly not in a position to give it. Mind you, mentally I wasn't in a good place either and my way of thinking was not all that clear. Sometimes I took encouragement the wrong way; I took it as if it came from a place of sorrow. People were encouraging me because they felt sorry for me. While I appreciated all the encouragement I received, who it came from sometimes left me wondering, why? Why were they encouraging me? Was there a hidden agenda behind this encouragement? Could I trust it and believe it to be genuine? I was very selective about who was encouraging me and what I was placing my hope in. I wanted to be familiar with who encouraged me and where I placed my hope and didn't want to try anything new. The people that encouraged me were not just saying what sounded good, they truly believed I could accomplish the goals I set to achieve.

There came a time when I needed others to talk about my struggles and applaud my efforts. I don't know why I needed this validation, but I did. I felt as though it placed value on my situation. When people made a big deal out of what I was attempting to do, it let me know that people actually cared about my well-being and that I mattered to them. I had a number of supporters who knew the direction I was trying to go. Being aware of my struggles, they were careful about the things they said around me and they were careful about what they did in my presence. Over a period of time once the word got out that I had stopped drinking, this became the reaction from just about everybody who knew me. I began receiving encouragement from people I knew of, and people I'd never associated with, people of prestige, educators, religious leaders, and community activists. These were the people that began to pour into me. Those that were encouraging me were showing me they were available to help make sure I had everything I needed to have a successful recovery. The generous amount of support I received helped me believe I could live my life without drinking. This encouraged me through rough times because these people believed in me and saw what I didn't see. This motivated me and allowed me to stay focused, work harder, and not give up on my dream.

If I told you I didn't entertain thoughts of relapsing, I'd be lying. Just like anyone trying to recover from an addiction, the thought of reusing was always present which is why having the right people around me to remind me that failure was not an option, was very important. I was aware that I was in a very critical place trying to recover. Only certain people had access to me, which were the ones who held me accountable and helped me push past negative thoughts. When I had those difficult moments, these key people helped me get past the challenges without accepting any excuses. In those moments I knew people cared for me and believed in me due to the amount of time they invested in me to make sure the journey ended with success. It was hard to believe there were people who were willing to invest their time and resources in me and to be positive influences for me. I was fortunate to have the right people positioned around me as my support system. They encouraged me to stay strong and fight through the struggles when I had urges to drink or I just needed someone to talk to.

I had dreams and desires; I envisioned myself being in a better place. I could see myself sober and functioning like a normal person; this encouraged me. At times though, I was an emotional roller coaster with more lows than highs. I found myself depressed a lot. When I did, I would often want to go back to my "happy place" under the influence of the bottle where no pain existed but I knew this was not an option. I wanted to drink because I was losing this battle and that was the only way I knew how to cope with failure and my emotions. What was controlling me was also trying to control my ability to release it. It was dictating my recovery. The addiction that had silently grown out of control over the years was aggressively trying to control my recovery.

Memories of my dad during this same period in his life were helping me most during this process because our struggles were similar. It wasn't long after my dad died that I had a dream that I was walking through a neighborhood I wasn't familiar with. In the dream my dad was walking with me. I remember crying and there was this older lady standing at the end of a driveway near the street and as we approached, she asked me, "Why are you walking and crying at the same time? Stop! Do one or the other!"

My then dad turned to me and said, "Whatever you do right here, don't stop! If you have to cry, cry. If you have to be angry, be angry. If you have to be sad, be sad. Whatever you have to deal with, deal with it, but don't stop! Your emotions will try to get the best of you and it may cause you to want to stop. If you stop, you might not have the strength to push through. You may not know how to start back and then you may give up. Deal with your problems and whatever emotions may be attached to them. Eventually, you will get where you desire to be."

Even though my drinking worsened after my dad's death, I always felt that through this dream my dad was encouraging me. My dad knew exactly how to keep things simple. It just took me some time to receive his warning because I was in denial. We are emotional beings and everything we deal with has our emotions attached to it. You can either control your emotions or let your emotions control you. What my dad was saying to me was I had to deal with the problems that I had to face and not stop in the midst of them, because if I stopped, I could give up in a place where I didn't want to be.

A lot of what my dad experienced, I was facing myself; the connection helped me a lot because I could relate and understood exactly how he felt trying to overcome something alone with no idea of how to do it. My dad had always been my hero. What made him a hero to me was his continuous fight against this horrible disease. My dad didn't allow the abuse to just happen to him. He kept fighting and never gave in. Even when I saw he was getting tired, he fought with what strength he had. What has motivated me the most was that my dad did not take alcoholism lying down; he fought it like a man, and as a man, he realized some battles couldn't be won. Even though society may have labeled him a "drunk", I thank God I was able to see the real him. A hero rose up within him, and he encouraged me, saying, "Son, be more than what you see in me." Unfortunately, his efforts did not get him the results he wanted, but for me, he would have wanted me to give it my all.

When I took my first drink I didn't know it would one day have me in the fight of my life. Looking back, I've come to realize that anything can be a giant in your life if you don't control it when it is small. I believe generational curses do exist, but I also believe that the curses can be broken. Growing up the son of an alcoholic was not easy. I remember in my teenage years people would say, "You'll be just like your dad". Well, the truth is, I wanted to be like my dad! He was a loving husband, good father, and proud of his sons. As a child I wasn't able to understand my dad's addiction and why it had him acting certain ways, but I know for a fact this is not something he would have wanted for any us. Even though I didn't understand why he acted the way he did or said the things he said, my dad was still my hero.

My dad had a Jekyll and Hyde personality; it was like the addiction was its own person. He was great as long as he wasn't under the influence. I hated the Hyde persona that would transform when he was under the influence. He was a good man that was possessed by a bad spirit. It was hard for my dad because though he wouldn't admit it, he was embarrassed to go around his family because of his problem. I remember as a child we would go to the rehabilitation center with my dad and stay the night to help motivate him. I can remember how the doctors would have the orderlies strap my dad to the bed to prevent him from walking out of the facilities or hurting himself or someone else. I remember there were times when I'd be home watching TV and would hear my dad in his bedroom talking, holding a conversation. When the phone would ring, I'd find out he was talking to himself. That's a lot for a child to see a parent go through. As a child over the years, I saw this addiction tare through my dad and physically I didn't see him do much to fight back.

The way I was trying to rehabilitate myself was similar to the way my dad had handled his situations–alone. I was trying to pattern my recovery after his lifestyle; it seemed to work for him. He would shut everything out as best he could and deal with the rest as it came. I know he didn't want to be a bother to anyone because of the distance he put between himself and others. He imprisoned himself in his addiction because this was how he felt he needed to deal with it. For a long time I'm sure my dad's side of the family may have thought we didn't want to have anything to do with them but that was not the case. Growing up, my dad isolated himself from his family and others because this is how he coped with his alcoholism–alone.

Even in his struggles, my dad was a proud man and he did his best to keep himself up as best he could. Over the years his condition worsened and his appearance began deteriorating. Eventually it was something that could no longer be hidden. There was no hiding the obvious. Prior to this state, I don't think any of his siblings knew what type of shape he was in; only my mom, my brothers, and I along with a few others.

His addiction didn't just affect him; we were all affected by it. He tried to internalize it because it was personal and private and that's how he dealt with it but externally, it affected all of us which I'm sure is why my mom didn't object to my dad's decision to stay away from the rest of the family. It was to preserve his image. I'm sure mom could have taken us to visit family without my dad but of course people would have asked questions that I'm sure my mother wouldn't have wanted to answer. For a long time this was something that I personally struggled with, wondering if anyone thought it was my mother that prevented us from being around family. She never wanted things to be that way, but I think she went along with it to preserve my dad's pride and dignity because he was really ashamed of his condition. My dad distanced himself because he was embarrassed; in his mind he began to look like he lived. This is why I did not want to rehabilitate myself by being isolated from the people that I loved and who truly loved me and were concerned about my well-being.

I believe my mother and Tina's journeys through alcoholism were different yet alike. Tina did not ask to be in a relationship with a man who had a drinking problem. But I certainly could not have asked for a better woman to be by my side during my struggle. It takes a strong person to stand beside someone you love when he suffers through something as debilitating as alcoholism. Though there may be many attempts to reach them, the problem could persist and get worse. If you're fortunate, your helpmate will stand with you as you take on this problem. My father and I were fortunate enough that they made a decision to remain in a relationship with us as we tried to overcome our illness. My mother made a decision and she exemplified the meaning of "for better or worse, in sickness and in health." In her decision my mother made sacrifices. I saw what it meant for someone to lose the one you loved while they were living. My mother gave until she was empty. She helped until it hurt and not one time did we ever hear her speak a negative word against our dad or make him feel less than a man because of his condition. She remained by my dad's side and was supportive and encouraging up until his death.

Tina's qualities were similar to my mother's in so many ways. Tina stuck by me when she didn't have to. My mother and father were joined together in Holy Matrimony, not making it quite as easy to call it quits, if she decided to. Tina and I were joined together by love and a verbal commitment. We loved each other and because of that, she committed to support me and my efforts to stop drinking as long as I committed to making progress and show her that I was working to make our relationship better. I worked to improve myself and I never went without being encouraged by her. Tina made sure I stayed involved by consulting me in all matters. I never lost my place as a man even when I was not able to contribute to our living arrangements. I didn't want for anything and when she had any extra to give, she gave, even offering to give to my children as well. I literally saw the very best come out of both Mom and Tina during the worst time, and still, they managed to gracefully maintain themselves, their households, and everything involved. It's very safe to say Tina had become my life coach because of the way she helped me and encouraged me to think carefully through my decisions and the steps I needed to get myself together. She gave me advice that made sense. What I accomplished over the next few days showed that I was definitely headed in the right direction but she still encouraged me to take it one day at a time. She was not an expert and she didn't have any type of training in being a life coach, but everything she said was different and it sounded right. I began depending on her advice and opinion.

I had success not drinking up to this point, but it wasn't such that I could walk out of that apartment and act like nothing had happened. The success was a great start but I couldn't rely on it enough to say I was cured. It would've been careless and extremely dangerous had I done that. During the second week I began to pay a big price for small successes. The bad dreams had returned by the end of the first week; I just didn't say anything to Tina or anyone else about it. The dreams had gotten so bad that I avoided sleeping at night out of fear. I was left confused because what I saw made no sense and left me wondering if I was going to be a physical threat to the woman and people I loved. When I dreamed I was physically violent towards Tina, that's when I knew I was going through detoxification. I was scared of course and for a number of reasons. To physically harm the woman who had loved and cared for me and had rescued me was something I could never see myself doing but in my dream I had handled Tina like she was nothing.

I had some difficult days in that apartment and I remember trying my best not to feel defeated. I tried not to think about all I was up against, what was ahead of me, and the consequences I had to face. I remember thinking about all the things I was going to be exposed to and how was I going to handle them. A few days of not drinking were good but not enough to say I was ready to go back into the world. Certainly, I hadn't stopped long enough to say I was ready to handle my tomorrow any differently than I was dealing with my yesterday. I was struggling and very afraid because I knew there would be consequences and that some of the consequences would have side effects. It was time to walk out of that apartment and I needed my surroundings to be different and new. I was still vulnerable and could have returned to what I was familiar with. Before Tina would leave for classes in the mornings, she would say to me, "Don't try to do too much at one time and if you don't feel comfortable doing it, then maybe it's too much." If I was going through with this, I had to deal with it; it couldn't be avoided because of the abuse I'd gone through. This attempt at rehabilitation was more mental than anything else.

ISOLATION

A S A CHILD, what I witnessed and heard about people going through rehabilitation was one of the biggest fears I faced. I was afraid of the chills, night sweats, hallucinations, and terrors. These were some of the physical side effects I could potentially face as a result of the detox. There were also the things that I would face in my head. There was the depression, anxiety, loneliness, and fight to not relapse. My body was in a fight with my head. I was at war. Mentally and physically there was a price to pay to be rehabilitated.

Somewhere on this road to recovery, the consequences of my actions would have to be faced. I've always viewed consequences as punishment or as some would say justified payback for wrongdoing. Although wrongs can be righted, and mercy can be shown, there are some consequences that can't be avoided. Even freedom from addiction, comes at a cost. The consequences that a person must face can be challenging, discouraging, and cause setbacks if you don't know how to deal with them. It was my belief that anyone wanting freedom from an addiction would go in one of three directions when facing consequences. Either they would go through with it, go back to it, or give up in the midst of it. It was not until I started talking to myself, rejecting sex, and lost my appetite that I realized it was I who was now facing the consequences of my actions.

The day I began talking to myself, my fear spiked to a whole new level. I was not generally in the habit of talking to myself, so I immediately knew something was wrong when I was engaged in a full length conversation. This was not the casual mumble under your breath type of talking to yourself that everyone does occasionally when you're trying to remember to set the alarm before you walk out of the door, or when you remind yourself to stop and pick up milk on your way home. These were question and answer sessions I was having with myself. These conversations were private and meant only for me. I was even going so far as to talk in third person. I knew I was tripping. I was scared but too afraid to call and tell anyone what was going on with me. During these talks the conversations went like,"Keith, why does it have to be so damn hard to stop drinking?" "I don't know, but it is. Man, I could really use a drink, but I know I shouldn't. It's getting hard Keith but don't do it. It's not worth it." These weren't just conversations I was having in my head. These were conversations I was having out loud taking me back to the times when I would hear my dad in the room having the same type of conversations with himself. Had someone walked in on me, they would have thought I was crazy and I might be back on my way to somebody's facility. It took me a minute to realize that I was doing it. But when I did, I was scared because I knew this wasn't normal. They hadn't prepared me for this at the rehab facility, so I was pretty sure at this point I was having a mental breakdown.

When I lost my desire for intimacy I knew something was wrong with me. My lack of desire for sex was a serious issue. I had never had any problems in this area before. It had nothing to do with Tina or my attraction to her. Our chemistry was still there, there was just something internally not connecting with me. Typically when we would go to bed, I would fall asleep with her back firmly to my chest holding her breasts in my hands with my head resting on her head. I knew something was wrong when I no longer wanted to hold Tina in this way. At the point that I went from not wanting to hold her at night, to not wanting to have sex at all, I knew things had gone from bad to worse. I had always had a high sex drive. I went from wanting sex all the time to not wanting it at all. Could sitting in that apartment for so long, going through what I was going through, while depriving my body of what it thirsted for be the reason I didn't want intimacy anymore? Tina could have thought the worst because I'm sure she noticed the change in my routine, but she didn't mention it.

I remembered sitting in front of the social worker while he explained to me some of the effects I was going to experience during treatment and how he would help me through these had I stayed at the facility. "Depression is a condition of the mind, not the position a person is in. How do you deal with depression?" he'd asked.

"I don't know; I just deal with it," I replied.

He responded, "No, you drink; that's how you've dealt with it. The first drink of the day is very important to an alcoholic because this is how they cope with their day and their depression."

He explained that an "Emotional Hangover" was the negative thoughts and opinions an alcoholic believed to be true about himself. Alcoholics would allow their first thoughts of the day regarding themselves to add to their depression. It was that emotional hangover that consumed my first thoughts as well, even before I got out of bed. I tried to make sense of it but I just couldn't understand why trying to quit something so bad was taking away something so good. It was not just good because it was sex, it was good because it was tied to Tina who my heart desired, yet this depressive state I was in had me not wanting to be involved with her or anyone else for that matter. I had no idea my mind and my desire for the physical touch were going to be affected the way they had been.

I was allowing my condition, and where I was mentally, to make my situation worse. In that apartment things were getting bad because my mind was deteriorating. What I hated most about dealing with my depression were the days I woke up already depressed. I felt like I had no purpose, no reason to live, and nothing to really push and motivate me to get past how I was feeling.

As a child I was an emotional eater, but somewhere between childhood and alcoholism, my appetite had been suppressed. I'm not sure if it was a result of the physical training in band camp or just swapping out one addiction for another, but I hadn't been much of an eater prior to admitting myself into rehab. Any little appetite I had after admission was now gone. How ironic was it that I had no appetite for food or intimacy, the two things in my life that I craved most outside of beer itself. I had missed a few meals before and survived, so that wasn't a big deal to me. My issue was that I had no desire for things that were vital to my existence. This is what made this scary. I really didn't know how to handle this dilemma. There had been times when I made the choice to drink before I ate but never did I get to a point where I had no desire to eat at all. But these were choices. I did not choose not to want to eat, or choose not to have sex, it came attached to the mental condition I was in. Again, this was a problem.

I chose to isolate myself in an attempt to stay away from distractions that could have led to stress and possibly cause me to relapse during my recovery. This was in an effort to try to change my mindset as the doctor had instructed; out of sight, out of mind. It was "a state of mind, not a position". Maybe there was something to removing from the physical that also removed from the mental as well. I had lost my desire for intimacy and for whatever reason my desire for the woman I loved was almost nonexistent as well. Maybe I had isolated myself to the point of total shutdown. There is no doubt that I had pushed myself further into a state of depression and the negative thoughts that accrued had definitely affected my behavior making my position appear worse than it actually was.

Mentally and physically I'm not sure how much more I could have taken being in that position. My mind wanted to keep me in a bad place because it was consumed with constant thoughts of failure. I was constantly thinking about the consequences of what would happen if I started back drinking. I knew first and foremost I would lose Tina. She was very adamant about her position. If I started drinking again she would leave, and I would have that to deal with as well. In addition, my relationships with my children were damaged because of drinking. My job situation was a complete mess. My finances were a nightmare. I had failed in all of these areas in my life because I had no control. To even consider going back to drinking was pointless because I already had so many things working against me. That wouldn't solve anything and would only make matters worse.

Being isolated made me feel like a caged animal that nobody wanted. I felt like a prisoner who had been sentenced to life and was about to walk the green mile. I couldn't think about success because the hope I had was slowly fading away; it was overshadowed by my current outlook which were conditions that I had placed myself in. The tortuous state was self-inflicted. My rationale for solitary confinement appeared to be good at the time, but it was currently working against me.

As I was sitting there in confinement and reflecting on what I was able to witness in those going through the treatment program at the rehab, encouraged me. I saw their focus and their work ethic, and I was able to see what was required to live and maintain without using. In the same light, it was also motivating to see those back who were trying to recover because I needed to see what failure looked like. Failure was real and was a part of recovery. In most cases, it almost always showed up at least once. I had to know what happened to those folks and why they were back so I could make sure that wouldn't be me. I hate to say it this way, but when I'd talked to people in rehab centers who'd tried quitting before and failed, it scared me because if they're back in, I'd think about my chances and wonder how do I prevent this from happening to me. Yes, sobriety was something I desired to have, but just the thought of re-entering into rehab because of failure really put fear in my heart. It seemed that I talked to more people that had failed than people who were successful. Although sad and discouraging, the possibility of failure sometimes keeps you on track for success. Sobriety wasn't going to be easy but it was something I would accomplish.

I was grateful for my time in rehab though short it was, because I was able to witness someone firsthand who had gone through the recovery process. It showed me that it doesn't matter what side of the table you sit on, to witness recovery, or live through it, wasn't easy. These people came out of rehab with high expectations, and most importantly, I'd like to think they believed in themselves. They believed that they could remain sober and live productive lives. I'm sure they envisioned themselves doing better and having more without being addicted to any type of substance. To have a quality of life meant the individual had to be clean…no exceptions!

The ones that failed (I assumed) probably went back into the environment they had come out of thinking they could pick up where they'd left off. They thought everything would be okay and that they could hang with the same people and visit the same places. Eventually this probably led to their relapses. Would this be me? Hell, why not? I fit the description; I was not exempt from relapse or failure, but in my mind I was better and I wanted to believe failure was not an option.

There was one thing I had to take into consideration, and truth be told, I had to think about it because the thought would not leave my mind. It was almost like being forced to think about my next move. Would I be strong enough to return to an environment where everything was easily accessible? I wanted to believe I could, but I couldn't stop thinking about those who had already tried and failed. Did they think they were strong enough before they entered their environments?

It's almost impossible to start out strong in a place where one was once extremely weak. It takes time to build strength. If you think you are strong enough to go back into an area where you were once weak you are setting yourself up for failure. It takes time to get stronger and in some cases, you don't fully recover. Some areas are too sensitive and some losses are too valuable to recover from. What I had to lose was definitely not worth going back to the neighborhood, seeing familiar faces, shooting the breeze, and facing the temptation. This type of loss had the potential to leave a person permanently weak and extremely vulnerable from the damage suffered in trying to transition back into society. I knew I wasn't strong enough to handle this and I would potentially not be able to recover from any damage I might sustain.

Society alone can be detrimental to recovery, and even people can serve as a source of weakness. When you add the wrong people at the wrong time, it can be fatal. Unfortunately, people can't be avoided in every situation when going back into society. Some of the people that we had dealings with prior to our removal can also be the same people that we have to deal with when we return. Change doesn't look the same to everyone, and unfortunately some people remain the same. A person had to be damn near spotless for me to go around them because I knew I was vulnerable, and could fall back into my old habits. I didn't need the temptation because I knew my vulnerabilities could win out. I didn't want to find myself sounding like others who were going through recovery saying, "I'm trying to stop drinking." That's an attempt and I get it; it is a struggle and every day is a test. There are trials. I couldn't always avoid being tempted and temptation was coming from every direction. I understood what it meant to try, but for me I did not need to hear myself speak "attempts". I had to hear my words speak action, "I can, through Christ, stop drinking!" That's what I had to hear, and it motivated and encouraged me through my struggles.

In that apartment I was fighting against the spirit of defeat when this scripture came into my spirit. I wasn't feeling the best; I guess I was still depressed and still trying to process what was going on and realizing there was no other place for me to face my situation. This was it; there was no going back. I had to trust what I felt. Trying to conquer something and not being properly prepared was going to be difficult but maybe this is why I began remembering portions of my dreams in rehab where I was told, "I've equipped you." I said to God, "If you don't do it, it won't get done." I kept pondering over that interaction. I didn't know it, but the words "I can" was what I needed to hear myself say.

To hear people say, "You can make it," helped, and it made a difference, but when I said it, it took on a whole new meaning. It came from a different place; it was coming from me. The words weren't just general concern; I actually felt positive about my situation, the outcome, and my life. That was something I hadn't been able to feel in a very long time. To finally be able to encourage myself in a situation that had controlled me for many years felt promising, and to hear myself speak an encouraging word like, "I can," gave me hope that I didn't know existed. I wanted to be hopeful, but I wasn't sure how to, and at that point, I began asking God to help me in my hope. I've always been told, "It's not how you start the race that'll determine the outcome, it's how you finish the race that counts." Every race is different and the emphasis should not be placed on finishing first or finishing ahead of someone because some races are not to be finished in a certain order. Some races are designed for us to just finish.

In order for me to finish this race, I had to put myself in a position to finish. Focus along with determination and a desire to have a better quality of life was my strategy and it was the only way I could see myself finishing the race successfully. During the process, I found it extremely helpful to disconnect from people who were constantly looking down on me because I did not measure up to their expectations. I had to distance myself from people who felt they could talk to me and treat me the way they wanted because they felt my addiction made me undeserving of respect. Clearly my addiction was noticeable. It was something I couldn't hide if I tried, but for people to see I had a problem and still treat me badly didn't encourage me at all. So I learned that investing in myself was extremely important. It came at a time when the only voice I heard was my own. I had to learn how to hear and recognize my own voice for encouragement. When the time came and no one else was trying to motivate me or make sure that I stayed in the race, I would have to depend on myself. I could no longer expect others to be on the sidelines cheering me on like my finish depended on them. It was my responsibility to finish the race, and it was my voice I needed to hear.

What does it say about the runner that started first and finished last? Was he not focused? Did he take his position for granted? He was qualified to be in the first position but he did not condition himself to maintain his place. So just because a person starts in a good place doesn't mean that person is going to have a good finish. People who are not able to start in a good place aren't necessarily destined to finish in a bad position. Starting out in the worst possible condition was discouraging, but thankfully, my circle of supporters made the difference. I had a support system that showed me how to care for myself and to stop dwelling over past failures and setbacks. Everything I'd encountered was helping me to get closer to the finish line. I was tired of being in the race to recover; I wanted it to be over. I was sick of hoping for a better life. I wanted it, but how was I going to get it?

When I made the commitment to better my life I made it regardless of how my conditions were at that time. I knew it was a bold statement given the current state of affairs, but I committed to improving my life even when the place I was in was not conducive to the outcome. I had a willingness and desire that things would be better than they were so I was going to work to ensure that I would make sure it happened. I had reasons to live better than the way I was living at the time. Hard or not, I was determined I was going to make it through it. I had convinced myself that I was going to accomplish this goal. No commitment would ever get accomplished without facing challenges. I was aware of the fact that when the doors opened to the apartment and I walked out, my fate would be determined by what happened on the outside. I had no other choice; I had to put all of this behind me.

During this time a transformation happened. I went from drinking for no reason, to telling myself I didn't need to drink, to not drinking at all. I went from being drunk every day, to having that last drink on the way to rehab, to not drinking for two weeks. I was a long way from where I started and to some this may be nothing but to me, this was a major accomplishment. This accomplishment did wonders for my self-esteem and it motivated me to prepare myself for what was to come.

For two weeks that apartment was my safe haven. I was secure. I was away from negative influences. I didn't even talk on the phone during my lock-in. When I say I had no access, I mean no access. I didn't need distractions and I only required what was important like support, encouragement, and love. In that apartment I only had access to the things I needed with no access to the things I wanted. My commitment was to be a better me. I spoke words that I knew would be challenged when I spoke them. They were words that made me stronger in character and built my confidence. That moment I opened the front door, I felt an array of challenges awaiting me but because of these two weeks I felt better than I had in a long time. Because of that, I was ready to face whatever had to come. I was not going to let anything or anyone hinder the progress I had made.

The world did not stop for me to get better, and it did not stop because I chose to stay in solitude for two weeks. The world didn't owe me anything. My commitment had to be accompanied by action. When I walked out of that apartment there was no turning back; I could no longer stay isolated because I knew there was going to come a time when the walls could no longer hold me and the works of my commitment had to begin. There was no such thing as pick up where you left off. I honestly believed I had to create a whole new beginning. To pick up something that I'd released could have been deadly and there was no need in going back to where I left off because there was nothing for me to return to. This was about a new beginning, a fresh start, and a new outlook!

A FRESH START

L EAVING MISSISSIPPI WAS good for me because it took me from an area where I was comfortable and moved me to an unfamiliar place where I had no connections. I didn't know anyone or anything about the area where I was going. This was a scary feeling. This was my first real experience away from home and family and all things familiar. There was nowhere to run if I needed to get away. There was no hanging out on the weekends because I didn't have friends there. No more family gatherings surrounded by food, laughter, and good times celebrating just about every holiday that you could possibly think of. Although, I was initially reluctant to go, God allowed the move to be a benefit to me. He led me to a place where I could heal; a place where I could find refuge in marriage.

Marriage had the kind of influence on me that I credit with saving my life. I didn't realize marriage could add so much value to my life; it was quite overwhelming. Marriage gave my life meaning and purpose. Marriage gave me something real that I could believe in, though it required work. It required me to think less of myself and more of my wife by putting her needs before my own. This was no easy task, but the fulfillment that it gave me and the positive change that it added was invaluable. It replaced all the negative things that were so harmful to me in my past.

Shortly after Tina and I were married, we moved to Raleigh, North Carolina. Initially, I was against it. I didn't want to go. I was being selfish in my hesitation to go even though the woman that I loved and had committed to, sacrificed so much on my behalf. How could I possibly say no to this request? This was one of her life's dreams. She put in the work and stayed focused despite it all. After all she had dealt with including me, she still graduated from college with honors and had landed a good job. This was the reward for all her efforts, and what was I going to say, "No, we're not going!" She had hoped to move away from home to a better place. What I didn't know was God allowed the better place to be the right place. I was scared but determined not to let my fears interfere with making this very important move. For a number of reasons I considered not going, but I wasn't looking for reasons, I was simply looking for excuses. I just didn't want to leave my comfort zone. I wanted us to live in Jackson, Mississippi but in reality, it was time for me to experience something new. I'll never forget the conversation with my mother about our moving. I wanted to make sure she would be okay and to my surprise her reaction wasn't quite what I'd expected, but it confirmed the move was right. She said "Keith, the time is right. You and Tina are fine to go. This is what she's worked hard for and it's time for you to go make a life for yourself. She's special and you'll be fine. I'll miss you guys but I love you son. I'll be fine. You don't need to worry about leaving me, I'm a big girl." The conversation with my mother made me feel better and a lot less worried about her when the time came for us to move.

I began to see God putting things in place and preparing us for the move. My biggest concern was if I had a buddy system or someone reliable should the urge to drink return. I wasn't one hundred percent confident that I wouldn't potentially relapse. I was doing really well with a few urges here and there but nothing really to be alarmed about. But I wanted to have someone available to help encourage me if I was faced with one of those difficult times that I didn't think I would get myself through.

Our marriage was no different than any other young couple starting out. We went through growing pains just like everyone else trying to adjust to married life. But we had to rely on each other for strength. We found that when in Mississippi, we could easily go find mama, and sisters, and brothers, and friends to be our sounding boards, but now, it was just us. We were each other's support. And although my biggest concern with moving was relapsing due to lack of a support system, my helpmate proved to be better than any buddy system could ever be. Tina's care for me and the way she helped and encouraged me through my transition was incomparable to what any friend or relative could have provided. As God would have it, my wife became all the support I needed.

Leaving Mississippi was a challenge and what made it more difficult was that I had a lot of idle time to think about the various stages of my life. I thought about what I'd experienced, what I overcame, and what I could have and should have done differently. All of this was weighing heavily on my mind. Initially, I cried a lot. I was depressed and bothered by my past and the fact that I wasn't where I needed to be at the time. I knew success was in my future, but it hadn't knocked on my door just yet. The heaviness was creeping back in and trying to turn into anger and it was the anger that I wasn't sure how to control. I began opening up to Tina about my struggles and my past, and the more I talked, the more she listened, and the less I cried. Sharing my innermost thoughts left me feeling vulnerable and I was concerned that what I shared would cause her to judge me or think less of me. Of all the things I shared, not one time did she utter a negative word, which allowed me to confide and share with her more freely.

I remember telling Tina I had wasted so much time and had nothing to show for it. I was down about it and I'm not sure if it was because I had to tell her I had wasted time or hadn't accomplished anything. I tried my best to release all of my anger, hurt, and hate from my past by confiding in Tina without draining her. I attempted to apologize for not having something to show for myself. I desperately wanted to be a strong contributor in our home but I wasn't quite there yet. As always, she found the right words to encourage me and rebuild me in my brokenness and simply said, "We will build together". I shared with her that I was struggling to wrap my mind around the concept of marriage and how difficult that was for me. In the beginning I had some doubts, not because I didn't believe in marriage. I was still struggling to believe the position I was in; it just took some time for me to believe my place in our marriage. What I was experiencing from Tina was too good to be true. I was afraid something in my past would cause this good thing to end but Tina assured me that as long as we stayed focused and stayed faithful, nothing could prevail against our marriage.

I started out thinking what was hers was hers and what was mine was mine. I didn't understand "togetherness" or "oneness" because I wasn't financially contributing so my interpretation at first was all wrong. I thought since I wasn't working that the personal bills that I brought into the marriage would have to wait until I got a job so I could pay them. I depended on her to take care of the bills we accumulated together. This is not how she thought of it and she made that clear. What we had, we had together. Old and new, it was all ours. This helped rid me of this selfish way of thinking.

Not long after we moved, I started having dreams again. These dreams were different. These dreams weren't like the ones from my childhood that had me afraid to sleep. Some of the dreams of my past involved scary images and dark places. These dreams weren't scary for any of those reasons; they were scary because I saw myself in a way I'd never seen before. In the dreams I saw myself preaching. The past I had didn't line up with the dreams I was having, so it was frightening. Clearly this wasn't the right dream; in fact, this was a bad dream. But why? I was finally focused on life and marriage; I was doing well with my sobriety and had no urges. I was finally in a good place, and then the dreaming began. I tried to ignore them but couldn't, and when I realized over time that the dreams hadn't stopped, it was obvious something was wrong.

There was a long list of preachers and prayer warriors in my family that came along before me. When my grandfather prayed, his prayers were so powerful; the foundation of the house would literally shake. *But me, preaching? How could this be?* The first time I had the dream, I saw myself in a white robe in a dark place, standing behind the podium and preaching. Those that I was preaching to looked like I did; they were lost and scared. The dreams woke me out of my sleep. I got up crying, not understanding what was happening. Why did I have this type of dream and of all people, why me? When it occurred, I woke up and went straight to my knees to pray. My prayer was silent because I didn't know what to say. I was shocked and in disbelief.

Things were going well with my life and marriage so I had a desire to know more about salvation and what it meant to live life as a Christian. The thought never crossed my mind about preaching though. Besides, from what I understood, God called those He wanted to preach and there was no way God was calling someone like me with a past like mine to preach anything. So that's exactly where my thoughts went. How could God want someone like me? I could barely read or write; I didn't speak well. I'd fathered children by different women out of wedlock, and I was still trying to recover from my past. Clearly, this was not the right dream. I wanted to know more about salvation. I was told salvation was for all, but preaching was not for me.

Now I didn't know how the calling thing worked, but I was not a candidate to stand in front of anybody and talk about God and living right. I desired salvation but just the thought of preaching scared me and I didn't want to have anything to do with it. The thought had never crossed my mind before but in the dream, it was clear that I was preaching.

I reached out to my former pastor back home in Mississippi, Reverend Dr. A. W. Crump Jr. to seek council from him regarding the dreams. He explained to me with a slight giggle, "God is a God of detail. What you have seen does not get any clearer than that. The dream can mean a number of things. Yes, it is possible God can be calling you to preach or calling you into some other type ministry, but the only way to get a definite answer is to talk to God. Pray and don't allow anybody to put a calling on you. Stay prayerful and spend time in God's word, and then the answer will settle well in your spirit."

I began noticing everything I was used to doing had totally changed. I was reading the Bible more. I was talking to people about the Bible and what I had read; I was very eager for knowledge. I was listening, learning, and not afraid to ask questions. The more I read the Bible, the more curious about it I became. After I received the advice from Dr. Crump, I didn't know where in the Bible to begin my research on how God called someone to preach. I went back to my go-to scripture from when I was in my recovery. All I could think about is what I said, what I did, and where I was when I said it. When I was in my transition, I quoted Philippians 4:13, "I can do all things through

Christ who strengthens me" several times a day, every day. Considering the challenges that were before me, why not go back to what worked?

It wasn't until I began studying Philippians 4:13 that my personal opinions about myself began to change. I stopped referring to myself as a failure, but as someone with a willing spirit with some limitations. God showed me he could work through those limitations and use even the unlikeliest of people to do his work. Just like Paul wasn't the most suitable candidate to be a preacher of the gospel, God could use me just as mightily as he had used him. It is said that God doesn't call the qualified. He qualifies the called. He doesn't necessarily choose those who are perfect or prepared; instead, he perfects or prepares those that he calls. I just didn't need to doubt my God-given abilities or let doubt hinder the works Christ could do through me.

Paul's situation was not ideal but he understood it was all a part of the process. I'm sure the process wasn't always easy to adjust to, but he stayed focused on the works that had to be done. His start did not determine how he would finish. If his beginning had told the story, his name would have never changed from Saul to Paul and he would not have been converted on the Damascus Road. Even though Paul was in prison, I'm convinced that this process was leading him to where he needed to be. It was later in my recovery that God allowed me to visualize the Apostle Paul in jail and I saw him in a very lonely place. The place he was being kept was designed to keep him isolated; there was no room for movement. It was to keep him from working in his purpose. He was confined to a situation that was intended to have a bad ending. But Paul spoke life despite the condition he was in and showed his determination not to allow his situation to dictate his outcome. He spoke with confidence and assurance that his position was a part of his process. What appeared to be bad and what looked gloomy would have a glorious ending.

In the apartment I'd come close to saying I didn't care. I'd come close to being a victim of my circumstances. I am thankful that even in my condition I was able to embrace my restored hope that one day I was going to experience something better than where I was. I'd come close to abandoning the vision because the conditions were not favorable. I had to understand that the responsibility fell on me to work in the conditions I was in if I wanted to accomplish my goal. If I had given up on my goals, I would have given up at a place in the process where I didn't want to be. There is nowhere written that says I will get in and out of this at the snap of a finger. The process could take a long time and this was one that I couldn't rush. Some people automatically think that if you're still stuck in the process and you've been there a long time, then you've failed. Towards the end of the process I was becoming frustrated, because I was close enough to see the end, but couldn't quite touch it. I needed that "can do" mentality to get me to the end although a "can do" mentality with no actions can hurt you. A "can do" mentality with no actions would have extended my process of recovery. I wouldn't have moved forward because acceptance would have become my excuse. When I learned Christ was my strength to accomplish what I desired, I had to stop saying what I "can do" and go ahead and get it done.

Something else I noticed about my visual visit with Paul was that he spoke as if he was already a free man. He didn't speak from his condition. Paul's condition affected him physically and left him with limited movement, but his condition didn't affect his spiritual outlook. I never would have thought God was allowing my past and the pain I endured to shape me for something greater than I could ever imagine. I made it through because God was with me the whole time. I didn't die in the process because God's hand was upon me. Who knew it would be through my struggles, my bad dreams, alcoholism, and adversities that God was preparing me to be a preacher? It was now however that I saw why God allowed me to have this visual of Paul, because when I saw Paul in his conditions, I saw myself. I saw myself incarcerated in dreams that scared me over half my life. They were dreams that had me afraid to speak out and ask for help. Physically I saw myself in places where I didn't want to be and mentally it was time for me to disconnect from my past that wanted to hurt, control, and keep me in fear. It was time to let go because I saw myself in a better place far greater than where I had been. To remain in the past, I would've been forcing myself to stay incarcerated. In *One Night*, love reached what addiction tried to kill. It reached my heart and soul and released me.

My life had been almost over and now it had been restored and what better way to show my appreciation than to yield to God's calling and preach of his goodness and saving power. I refused to have gone through all I'd been through to come out with a negative spirit and a bad attitude. I refused to not tell somebody that God did it. I refused not to tell somebody about the saving power of Jesus Christ. I refused to not tell somebody Jesus is the way the truth and the light. I'm thankful for the good things Tina saw in me and for not allowing anyone to influence her decision to be with me. What God did through the love of one woman convinced me that life was worth living. Because of my condition, I felt unlovable and because of my condition there was no need to have faith in anything. Conditions can kill possibility especially when you don't have faith to believe you're going to come out of it. Because of this encounter, the purest gift had been restored. Without love, why live? Without faith, why hope?

It was Paul who said in Philippians 3:13-14, "Brethren, I do not count myself to have apprehended; but one thing I do, forgetting those things which are behind and reaching forward to those things which are ahead, I press toward the goal for the prize of the upward call of God in Christ Jesus". Reflecting on all the things of my past has kept me humble. Humility is not just a word; it's my lifestyle. Everything I do, I do it in the spirit of humility because I know God has blessed me with another chance that someone else in a similar situation didn't get. Humility has kept me from developing the wrong attitude. It has helped when I wanted to get in my feelings and in the process helped me understand I am here for a purpose. I humbly seek God in all things and in everything I give Him glory.

My past did not happen by accident or mistake. It's my history and it is what makes me who I am now. One thing I found out about God is that He is persistent and what God's will is for your life, it will happen. It was early on a Thursday morning about two forty-five. I couldn't think straight and every thought took me back to my first dream of preaching. I still remember how terrified I was of it because I didn't understand the details and why. I had become more afraid of preaching dreams than I was of the dreams of my past. I was afraid because I couldn't see it happening. No one knew at the time that I was ignoring God's voice; I was not under an assumption that I was going to preach. I knew God had called me to preach. Finally I couldn't take it anymore. I told God that I'd heard Him for a long time and wrestled with my calling. God took me back to that one night in the rehabilitation room when He said,

"Not only have I given you what you need to remain sober, but I've also given you what you need to stand and preach my word. I called you out so that others can see my saving power." It was then that I said yes and surrendered to God's calling to preach.

Through the gift of love I was encouraged to fight through my struggles without excuses. Yes, it was a difficult journey but to God be the glory–I made it. My bad dreams and the addiction were forces too powerful for me to fight alone. I wanted to be in love more than I wanted to be in pain. In fact, I tried to love anything to hide my pain but what I loved was not giving me the same. In my struggles I saw someone that appeared to be out of place. She really didn't belong in the moment I was in. To see someone so beautiful during a time in my life that was bad wasn't unheard of, but for me, this kind of thing didn't happen. She caught my attention and it's not to say she enticed me but she was beauty in my bad place and her spirit couldn't be resisted. In seeing her, God showed me he required my attention. The language was different. She was so beautiful that I listened.

Was it God really talking to me by showing me something so beautiful in a place that was so bad? I remember saying,

> "God, I'm not sure what You're saying but please be clear and let me hear You because the beauty that You've placed before me is drawing me near. It is You who holds the future. If You will allow me tomorrow and then extend it to forever, I will love her with my soul. God, I'm not sure what I have to do to come out of this place. I am reaching for You, please save me by Your grace. What I've experienced, You've allowed it to be. What I've faced, You've allowed me to see. God, only You hold the miracle I desire to be. Please open up this place and set me free."

My *one night* experience was a personal encounter with God. I experienced God in a very real way. My bad dreams and my struggles as a kid that carried into adulthood, I experienced them to help someone who is in that place where I once was. I was having a conversation with my cousin Overseer K. Ware and he told me, "God allows us to go through things that aren't for us. It's for us to help those who will come along behind us." I often think about that conversation and how God allowed this to happen so that I can help someone that might not know who they can call on or who they can trust. I want to let them know they have nothing to be ashamed of and encourage them to think above their current situation. I am so thankful for my children who I don't mind telling where I've been if it will prevent them from going down the same path. I thank God for blessing me to strive to be the best that I can be for them and I want to always remind them that a bad chapter can end well. I'm thankful God has blessed me to rise above my faults and do my best to right my wrongs.

This year of 2017, I celebrate twenty years of sobriety and there's not a day that goes by that I don't thank God for what He has done. I'm able to share my testimony because God has kept me. It is because of God's favor that I made it this far. What made the difference in my life is when I asked Jesus to be my Lord and Savior. If he has the ability to reach down and pull me from the hell I was in, he can do the same for anyone else with the same struggles. You're never too far gone to be saved. To my beautiful wife, my wonderful children, my mother, my brothers and all of my family and friends–I love each of you. It is my sincere prayer that you will not give up in your situations.

Constantly I've asked God, "why me?" God,

> *"Why did You allow me to experience so much at a young age and why did You allow my dreams to take me into dark places? Why did You allow me to face what I faced and not resemble any of the things of my past? You allowed it to be so that I may help someone else. Thank you because what You allowed is what has molded me to be who I am today. God, if I had the ability to change one thing about my past, I wouldn't dare touch a thing because nothing from my past haunts me. The alcoholic, You made sober. The deadbeat dad, You've now blessed to be a Father. Thank you for Special Education and being limited, but being limited didn't mean I couldn't excel. You allowed Satan to introduce alcohol to me and even that brought out a testimony in me. Thank you because it's all part of my past and it has shaped me to be who I am. I embrace my past and I thank you for it. I am an overcomer. I am a man of God! God, as I walk in this season, my desire is to remain humble and never get beside myself because I am tremendously blessed.*

God, please don't ever let me get away from a humble lifestyle. Everything I do, everything I say, and all that I am, humility is a part of it. God, You know I've never really understood what transparency meant, but I am thankful that I'm not ashamed to testify to be a witness to Your goodness to tell somebody what You have done and how You saved me. You delivered me and You set me free. God, You brought me through and brought me out and I know I'm not the same. If that's transparency then God, to You be the glory for allowing somebody to see through my past that You are an amazing God! I want a child to be delivered from whatever has them in bondage. God, my prayer is that the right people and the right resources are placed around any children dealing with these same situations. Help them to know You and your beloved son, Jesus, as their Savior. My prayer is that the alcoholic or someone addicted to drugs know that deliverance and help are available and that it's theirs for the asking. God, show me where to place my hands; God show me how and who I can help. God, thank you for trusting me with a past that wasn't pretty or perfect because, God it has shaped me into the man I am today. Thank you, God, for that One Night!

Printed in the United States
By Bookmasters

Printed in the United States
By Bookmasters